PROMETHEUS RISING

OTHER BOOKS BY ROBERT ANTON WILSON

* Published by Falcon Press

PROMETHEUS RISING

BY

Robert Anton Wilson, Ph.D.

Introduced
By
Israel Regardie

1992
NEW FALCON PUBLICATIONS
PHOENIX, ARIZONA U.S.A.

International Standard Book Number: 0-56184-056-4
Library of Congress Catalog Card Number: 83-81665

First Edition 1983
Second Printing 1984
Third Printing 1986
Fourth Printing 1987
Fifth Printing 1989
Sixth Printing 1990
Seventh Printing 1992

Cover by Stan Slaughter

New Falcon Publications
655 East Thunderbird
Phoenix, Arizona 85022 U.S.A.
(602) 246-3546

CONTENTS

Other Controversial Titles From New Falcon Publications

DEDICATED

To
Kurt Smith
Timothy Leary
&
G.I. Gurdjieff
dove sta memora

ACKNOWLEDGEMENTS

The eight-circuit model of consciousness in this book derives from the writings of Dr. Timothy Leary, whose letters and conversations have also influenced many other ideas herein. I also owe great debts to Dr. O.R. Bontrager, for introducing me to semantics and communication sciences generally; to R. Buckminister Fuller, for general sociological technological perspectives on current problems; and to all of the following: Barbara Hubbard, Alan Harrington, F.M. Esfandiary, Dr. Paul Watzlavik, Dr. Eric Berne, Dr. Paul Segall, Dr. Israel Regardie, Alvin Toffler, Phil Laut, Dr. Sigmund Freud, Dr. Carl Jung, Alan Watts, Alfred Korzybski, and Aleister Crowley. The members of the Physics/Consciousness Research Group (Dr. Jack Sarfatti, Dr. Nick Herbert and Saul Paul Sirag) have contributed more than is indicated by my few brief references to quantum theory in these pages; they clarified my whole comprehension of epistemology.

None of these persons are responsible for my mistakes or over-statements.

INTRODUCTION

By Israel Regardie

The ability to create a synthesis of diverse points of view, scientific and social and philosophical, is a rare gift. Not many are there who dare even to attempt such a task. Imagine anyone trying to make sense of an amalgam of Timothy Leary's eight neurological circuits, Gurdjieff's self-observation exercises, Korzybski's general semantics, Aleister Crowley's magical theorems, the several disciplines of Yoga, Christian Science, relativity and modern quantum mechanics, and many other approaches to understanding the world around us! A man is required with an almost encyclopedic education, an incredibly flexible mind, insights as sharp as those whom he is trying synthesize and *mirabile dictu*, a wonderful sense of humor.

For several years -- ever since I first became familiar with the writings of Robert Anton Wilson -- I have been struck with his ever-present sense of bubbling humor and the wide scope of his intellectual interests. Once I was even so presumptuous as to warn him in a letter that his humor was much too good to waste on the hoi polloi who generally speaking would not understand it and might even resent it. However this effervescent lightness of heart became even more apparent in *The Cosmic Trigger* and more latterly in the trilogy of *Schrödinger's Cat*. I have sometimes wondered whether his extraordinarily wide range of intellectual roving is too extensive and therefore perplexing to the average reader. Be that as it may, the humor and synthesis are even more marked in this brilliant ambitious piece of writing, *Prometheus Rising*.

Even if your reading has already made you familiar with some of the concepts employed by Wilson in this book, nonetheless his elucidation even of the simplest, the most basic, is illuminating. At this moment, I am referring to the "imprint" theory which he makes considerable use of. Much of the same is true of his references to and explanation of Leary's eight neurological circuits. We become familiar with them all over again, as if they had not been introduced to us before.

I

Moreover I love the subtle and almost invisible use of mystical dogma that permeates all his writings. For example, consider the opening of Chapter Six. It quotes a particularly meaningful sentence from William S. Burroughs. There is no mention -- nor need there be -- of any anterior teaching regarding this Law of Three, as it may be called. But one doctrine that emanated from a mediaeval mystical school philosophizes that there are always two contending forces -- for the sake of convenience labelled Severity and Mildness -- with a third that always reconciles them. It is paramount to this doctrine, which has been stated and stated again in a dozen or more different ways throughout the centuries, culminating finally in the idea enunciated by Burroughs and of course used by Wilson.

There are dozens of similar seeds of wisdom sown throughout *Prometheus Rising* that are bound to have a seminal effect wherever and whenever the book is read. This is one of the many virtues of Wilson's book; it will leave its mark on all those who read it -- and those seeds will surely take root and bloom in the most unlikely minds -- as well as in the more prosaic. Tarot advocates will find the most unusual and illuminating interpretations of some of their favorite cards when he falls back on the basic neural circuits. I found them all illuminating as providing a new viewpoint which had to be integrated into my general view of such matters.

The only area where I was reluctantly inclined to be at odds with Wilson was in what I considered to be his addiction to a Utopia -- which he eloquently enough expresses as "the birth pangs of a cosmic Prometheus rising out of the long nightmare of domesticated primate history." The history of mankind is also the history of one Utopia after another, being enunciated with enthusiasm and vigor, calling upon all the facts of faith and science (as they existed at that moment in space-time) to corroborate the fantasy. A decade or maybe a century elapse -- and the fantasy is no more. The Utopia has gone down the drain to join all the other Utopias of earlier primates. However, I sincerely hope that Wilson is *right* in this case.

Now I am not unmindful of the fact that the Utopia of which Wilson speaks, echoing many of the best scientific and philosophic minds of our day, is a distinct possibility at *some time*, but that it could occur within the next decade seems rather improbable to me. It seems improbable of course only in terms of the current state of world enlightenment, or lack of it, and because it implies a "miracle" occurring in vast numbers of living primates simultaneously -- whatever semantic theories are involved in the meaning of the word "simultaneously." Anyway, this is a minor point considering the seminal brilliance of the greater part of this enlightening book. In a previously written book, Wilson wrote that in "1964, Dr. John S. Bell published a demonstration that still has the physicists reeling. What Bell seemed to prove was that quantum effects are 'non-local' in Bohm's sense; that is, they are not just here or there, but both. What this apparently means is that space and time are only real to our mammalian sense organs; they are not *really* real."

This writing reminds me so much of the Hindu concept of Indra's Net. The latter is sometimes described as being a great net extending throughout the whole universe, vertically to represent time, horizontally to represent space. At each point where the threads of this Indra's net cross one another is a diamond or a crystal bead, the symbol of a single existence. Each crystal bead reflects on its shining surface not only every other bead in the whole net of Indra but every single reflection of every reflection of every other bead upon each individual bead -- countless, endless reflections of one another. We could also liken it to a single candle being placed in the centre of a large hall. Around this hall tens of mirrors are arranged in such a manner that, when the candle was lit, one saw not only its reflection in each individual mirror, but also the reflections of the reflections in every other mirror repeated *ad infinitum*.

One of the several virtues of *Prometheus Rising* is that Wilson using Leary's neurological circuits believes that a new philosophical paradigm is about due. In reality, this is really Wilson's answer to my proposed criticism of his Utopian fantasy. It may not be within a decade that we shall realize whether it is true or false. But that is not important. What is clear is that thanks to the insights of many modern thinkers, major new intellectual findings do not come solely from the slow drip and grind of tiny new discoveries, or from new theories simply being added to our present armamentarium of time-honoured truisms. Rather, quantum leaps, in outlook ala Teilhard de Chardin, occur with a fantastic jump to a new horizon or level of perception. This insight usually comes from a revolutionary *overview* which realigns or transforms former thinking into a new and more enlightening frame of reference.

This dovetails with his equally fascinating thesis that everything alive is really *alive* in the fullest and most dynamic sense of the word. It twitches, searches, throbs, organizes and seems aware of an upward movement. Twitches seems almost the right word, recalling to mind the myoclonisms of Wilhelm Reich's vegetotherapy which, at sometime, are infinitely disturbing to the patient on the couch who, because of them, feels he is falling apart, being shattered into a thousand pieces. He isn't really. It is as though the organism were gathering itself together for an upward or forward leap into the unknown, to a higher order of looking at things.

The transition to a higher order of functioning -- or hooking on to a higher neural circuit -- is often accompanied by considerable anxiety or a turbulence in personal life which seems as if the organism were falling apart or breaking up. This phenomenon of instability is really the way that every living organism -- societies, human primates, chemical solutions, etc. -- shakes itself, as it were, by myoclonisms or similar convulsions into new combinations and permutations for higher and new levels of development. So perhaps the space-time Utopia of a new area of primate exploration has some validity after all, as indicating that the more vigorous the disturbance or myoclonism the greater the quantum jump into a higher neurological circuit. This is one reason why I firmly believe that the transition to the next spiral will not be smooth nor without much suffering and chaos.

All of which suggests, with Wilson and Leary, that the brain is considerably more sophisticated than any of us previously had imagined. It is quite possible that it operates in dimensions so beyond the lower neural circuitry that it occasionally "throws us a bone" every day so that we can continue to function in the make-believe world of everyday status quo. In the meantime, it is a multidimensional structure at ease in far more than the narrow primate world we have been programmed to live in. It may interpret waves and frequencies from other dimensions, realms of "light", of meaningful unrestricted patterned reality -- that are here and now -- and which transcend our present myopic tunnel realities of our rigid perceptions and conceptualizations of space and time.

If so, then the title of this book *Prometheus Rising* is

INTRODUCTION

representative of more than a catchy title to a profound fascinating book. It becomes a title, instead, to the very attempt which we are now making to reach beyond ourselves with a quantum leap into a new world which has been envisaged only by a very few. Wilson is one of this group who are preparing themselves and if we allow them, the rest of us, to take our place in the New Aeon.

I will close with a quote from Wilson, "We are all giants, raised by pygmies, who have learned to walk with a perpetual mental crouch. Unleashing our full stature -- our total brain power -- is what this book is all about."

Israel Regardie
Phoenix Arizona
July 1983

CHAPTER ONE

THE THINKER AND THE PROVER

All that we are is the result of all that we have
thought. It is founded on thought. It is based
on thought.

Buddha, The Dhammapada

William James, father of American psychology, tells of meeting an old lady who told him the Earth rested on the back of a huge turtle.

"But, my dear lady," Professor James asked, as politely as possible,"what holds up the turtle?"

"Ah," she said, "that's easy. He is standing on the back of another turtle."

"Oh, I see," said Professor James, still being polite. "But would you be so good as to tell me what holds up the second turtle?"

"It's no use, Professor," said the old lady, realizing he was trying to lead her into a logical trap. "It's turtles-turtles-turtles, *all the way!*"

Don't be too quick to laugh at this little old lady. All human minds work on fundamentally similar principles. Her universe was a little bit weirder than most but it was built up on the same mental principles as every other universe people have believed in.

As Dr. Leonard Orr has noted, the human mind behaves as if it were divided into two parts, the Thinker and the Prover.

The Thinker can think about virtually anything. History shows that it can think the earth is suspended on the backs of infinite turtles or that the Earth is hollow, or that the Earth is *floating in space*;* comparative religion and philosophy show that the Thinker can regard itself as mortal, as immortal, as both mortal and immortal (the reincarnation model) or even as non-existent (Buddhism). It can think itself into living in a Christian universe, a Marxist universe, a scientific-relativistic universe, or a Nazi universe -- among many possibilities.

As psychiatrists and psychologists have often observed (much to the chagrin of their medical colleagues), the Thinker can think itself sick, and can even think itself well again.

The Prover is a much simpler mechanism. It operates on one law only: Whatever the Thinker thinks, the Prover proves.

To cite a notorious example which unleashed incredible horrors earlier in this century, if the Thinker thinks that all Jews are rich, the Prover will prove it. It will find evidence that the poorest Jew in the most run-down ghetto has hidden money somewhere.

*Millions of people believe that (including the present author).

If the Thinker thinks that the sun moves around the earth, the Prover will obligingly organize all perceptions to fit that thought; if the Thinker changes its mind and decides the earth moves around the sun, the Prover will re-organize the evidence.

If the Thinker thinks "holy water" from Lourdes will cure its lumbago, the Prover will skillfully orchestrate all signals from the glands, muscles, organs etc. until they have organized themselves into good health again

Of course, it is fairly easy to see that other people's minds operate this way; it is comparatively much harder to become aware that one's own mind is working that way also.

It is believed, for instance, that some men are more "objective" than others. (One seldom hears this about women . . .). Businessmen are allegedly hard-nosed, pragmatic and "objective" in this sense. A brief examination of the dingbat politics most businessmen endorse will quickly correct that impression.

Scientists, however, are still believed to be objective. No study of the lives of the great scientists will confirm this. They were as *passionate,* and hence as prejudiced, as any assembly of great painters or great musicians. It was not just the Church but also the established astronomers of the time who condemned Galileo. The majority of physicists rejected Einstein's Special Relativity Theory in 1905. Einstein himself would not accept anything in quantum theory after 1920 no matter how many experiments supported it. Edison's commitment to direct current (DC) electrical generators led him to insist alternating current (AC) generators were unsafe for years after their safety had been proven to everyone else.*

Science achieves, or approximates, objectivity not because the individual scientist is immune from the psychological laws that govern the rest of us, but because scientific method -- a group creation -- eventually over-rides individual prejudices, in the long run.

To take a notorious example from the 1960s, there was a point

*Edison's pigheadedness on this matter was partly the result of his jealousy against Nikola Tesla, inventor of A-C generators. Tesla, on the other hand, refused the Nobel Prize when it was offered to him and Edison *jointly* because he refused to appear on the same platform with Edison. Both of these geniuses were only capable of "objectivity" and science in certain, limited laboratory conditions. If you think you have a higher "objectivity quotient" than either of them, why haven't you been nominated for a Nobel prize?

when three research groups had "proven" that LSD causes chromosome damage, while three other groups had "proven" that LSD has no effect on the chromosomes. In each case, the Prover had proved what the Thinker thought. Right now, there are, in physics, 7 experiments that confirm a very controversial concept known as Bell's Theorem, and two experiments that refute Bell's Theorem. In the area of extra-sensory perception, the results are uniform after more than a century: everybody who sets out to prove that ESP exists succeeds, and everybody who sets out to prove that ESP does not exist also succeeds.

"Truth" or relative truth emerges only after decades of experiments by thousands of groups all over the world.

In the long run, we are hopefully approximating closer and closer to "objective Truth" over the centuries.

In the short run, Orr's law always holds:

Whatever the Thinker thinks, the Prover will prove. *

And if the Thinker thinks passionately enough, the Prover will prove the thought so conclusively that you will never talk a person out of such a belief, even if it is something as remarkable as the notion that there is a **gaseous** vertebrate of astronomical heft ("GOD") who will spend all eternity torturing people who do not believe in his religion.

EXERCIZES

Sad as it is to say, you never understand anything by merely reading a book about it. That's why every science course includes laboratory experiments, and why every consciousness-liberation movement demands practise of yogas, meditations, confrontation techniques, etc. in which the ideas are tested in the laboratory of your own nervous system.

The reader will absolutely *not* understand this book unless he or she does the exercizes given at the end of each chapter.

To explore the Thinker and the Prover, try the following:

1. Visualize a quarter *vividly,* and imagine *vividly* that you are going to find the quarter on the street. Then, look for the quarter every time you take a walk, meanwhile continuing to visualize it. See how long it takes you to find the quarter.

2. Explain the above experiment by the hypothesis of "selective attention" -- that is, *believe* there are lots of lost quarters everywhere and you were bound to find one by continually looking. Go looking for a second quarter.

3. Explain the experiment by the alternative "mystical" hypothesis that "mind controls everything." *Believe* that you made the quarter manifest in this universe. Go looking for a second quarter.

4. Compare the time it takes to find the second quarter using

---

*If the reader is a scientist, be not alarmed. This refers not to you but only to those benighted fools in the opposite camp who refuse to recognize that your theory is the only reasonable one. Of course.

the first hypothesis (attention) with the time it takes using the second hypothesis (mind-over-matter).

5. With your own ingenuity, invent similar experiments and each time compare the two theories -- "selective attention" (coincidence) vs. "mind controls everything" (psychokinesis).

6. Avoid coming to any strong conclusions prematurely. At the end of a month, re-read this chapter, think it over again, and still postpone coming to any dogmatic conclusion. *Believe it possible that you do not know everything yet, and that you might have something still to learn.*

7. Convince yourself (if you are not already convinced) that you are ugly, unattractive and dull. Go to a party in that frame of mind. Observe how people treat you.

8. Convince yourself (if you are not already convinced) that you are handsome, irresistible and witty. Go to a party in that frame of mind. Observe how people treat you.

9. This is the hardest of all exercizes and comes in two parts. *First,* observe closely and dispassionately two dear friends and two relative strangers. Try to figure out what their Thinkers think, and how their Provers methodically set about proving it. *Second,* apply the same exercize to yourself.

If you think you have learned the lessons of these exercizes in less than six months, you haven't really been working at them. With real work, in six months you should be just beginning to realize how little you know about everything.

10. Believe it possible that you can float off the ground and fly by merely willing it. See what happens.

If this exercize proves as disappointing to you as it has to me, try number 11 below, which is *never* disappointing.

11. Believe that you can exceed all your previous ambitions and hopes in all areas of your life.

ALL MODELS ARE SUBJECT TO REVISION AS THIS BOOK GOES ALONG. THEY ARE ALSO SUBJECT TO REVISION AFTER THE BOOK IS FINISHED -- BY THE AUTHOR OR BY THE READER.

Tenative Model #1: The perceived univcrse is a mixture of the "real universe" and our own "Thinker" -- proving it's pet beliefs.

CHAPTER TWO

HARDWARE AND SOFTWARE: THE BRAIN AND ITS PROGRAMS

We, as a species, exist in a world in which exist a myriad of data points.* Upon these matrices of points we superimpose a structure** and the world makes sense to us. The pattern of the structure originates within our biological and sociological properties.***

Persinger and Lafreniere,
Space-Time Transients and Unusual Events

*In our terminology, these data points are events or actions, i.e. verb, not nouns.
**In our terminology, models or maps, static things; nouns not verbs.
***In our terminology, brain hardware and software.

We will, throughout this book, consider the human brain a kind of bio-computer -- an electro-colloidal computer, as distinct from the electronic or solid-state computers which exist outside our heads.

Please note carefully and long remember that we have not said that the human brain *is* a computer. The Aristotelian idea that to understand something you must know what it *is* has been abandoned in one science after another, for the pragmatic reason that the simple word "is" introduces so many metaphysical assumptions that we can argue forever about them. In the most advanced sciences, such as mathematical physics, nobody talks about what anything *is* anymore. They talk about what *model* (or map) can best be used to understand whatever we are investigating.

In general, this scientific habit of avoiding "is" can be profitably extended to all areas of thought. Thus, when you read anywhere that A *is* B, it will clarify matters if you translate this as "A can be considered as, or modelled by, B."

When we say *A is B,* we are saying that A is *only* what it appears within our field of study or our area of specialization. This is saying too much. When we say *A can be considered as B,* or *modelled by B*, we are saying exactly as much as we have a right to say, and no more.

We therefore say that the brain can be considered as a computer; but we do not say it *is* a computer.

The brain appears to be made up of matter in electro-colloidal suspension (protoplasm).

Colloids are pulled together, toward a condition of *gel*, by their surface tensions. This is because surface tensions pull all glue-like substances together.

Colloids are also, conversely, pushed apart, toward a condition of *sol,* by their electrical charges. This is because their electrical charges are similar, and similar electrical charges always repel each other.

In the equilibrium between *gel* and *sol*, the colloidal suspension maintains its continuity and life continues. Move the suspension too far toward gel, or too far toward sol, and life ends.

Any chemical that gets into the brain, changes the gel-sol balance, and "consciousness" is accordingly influenced. Thus, potatoes are, like LSD, "psychedelic" -- in a milder way. The changes in consciousness when one moves from a vegetarian diet to an omnivorous diet, or vice-versa, are also "psychedelic."

13

Since "What the Thinker thinks, the Prover proves," all of our ideas are psychedelic. Even without experimenting with diet or drugs, whatever you think you should see, you *will* see -- unless it is physically impossible in this universe.

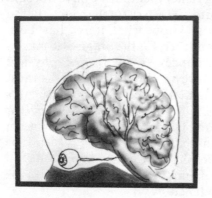

THE BRAIN IS NOT A COMPUTER

BUT THE BRAIN CAN BE MODELLED BY A COMPUTER

PLEASURE   PAIN   (INPUT)

PROGRAMS RUNNING

APPROACH   FLEE   (OUPUT)

All experience is a muddle, until we make a model to explain it. The model can clarify the muddles, but the model is never the muddle itself. "The map is not the territory"; the menu does not taste like the meal.

Every computer consists of two aspects, known as hardware and software. (Software here includes information).

The hardware in a solid-state computer is concrete and localized, consisting of central processing unit, display, keyboard, disk drive etc. -- all the parts you can drag into Radio Shack for repair if the computer is malfunctioning.

The software consists of programs that can exist in many forms, including the totally abstract. A program can be "in" the computer in the sense that it is recorded in the CPU or on a disk which is hitched up to the computer. A program can also exist on a piece of paper, if I invented it myself, or in a manual, if it is a standard program; in these cases, it is not "in" the computer but can be put "in" at any time. But a program can be even more tenuous than that; it can exist only in my head, if I have never written it down, or if I have used it once and erased it.

The hardware is more "real" than the software in that you can always locate it in space-time -- if it's not in the bedroom, somebody must have moved it to the study, etc. On the other hand, the software is more "real" in the sense that you can smash the hardware back to dust ("kill" the computer) and the software still exists, and can "materialize" or "manifest" again in a different computer.

(Any speculations about reincarnation at this point are the responsibility of the reader, not of the author.)

In speaking of the human brain as an electro-colloidal bio-computer, we all know where the hardware is: it is inside the human skull. The software, however, seems to be anywhere and everywhere. For instance, the software "in" my brain also exists outside my brain in such forms as, say, a book I read twenty years ago, which was an English translation of various signals transmitted by Plato 2400 years ago. Other parts of my software are made up of the software of Confucius, James Joyce, my second-grade teacher, the 3 Stooges, Beethoven, my mother and father, Richard Nixon, my various dogs and cats, Dr. Carl Sagan, and anybody and (to some extent) *any-thing* that has ever impacted upon my brain. This may sound strange, but that's the way software (or information) functions.

Of course, if consciousness consisted of nothing but this undifferentiated tapioca of timeless spaceless software, we would have no individuality, no center, no Self.

We want to know, then, how out of this universal software ocean a specific person emerges.

What the Thinker thinks, the Prover proves.

Because the human brain, like other animal brains, acts as an electro-colloidal computer, not a solid-state computer, it follows the same laws as other animal brains. That is, the programs get into the brain, as electro-chemical bonds, in discrete quantum stages.

Each set of programs consists of three basic parts:

1. *Imprints.* These are more-or-less hard wired programs which the brain is genetically designed to accept *only* at certain points in its development. These points are known, in ethology, as times of *imprint vulnerability*.

2. *Conditioning.* These are programs built onto the imprints. They are looser and fairly easy to change with counter-conditioning.

3. *Learning.* This is even looser and "softer" than conditioning.

In general, the primordial *imprint* can always over-rule any subsequent conditioning or learning. An imprint is a species of software that has become built-in hardware, being impressed on the tender neurons when they are peculiarly open and vulnerable.

Imprints (software frozen into hardware) are the non-negotiable aspects of our individuality. Out of the infinity of possible programs existing as potential software, the imprint establishes the limits, parameters, *perimeters* within which all subsequent conditioning and learning occurs.

YOUR HARDWARE IS LOCALIZED: BRAIN CELLS RIGHT HERE, RIGHT NOW.

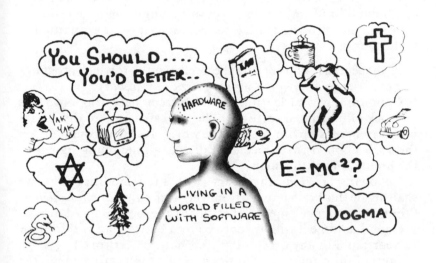

YOUR SOFTWARE IS NON-LOCAL: POINT-EVENTS EVERYWHERE, EVERYWHEN.

Before the first imprint, the consciousness of the infant is "formless and void" -- like the universe at the beginning of *Genesis,* or the descriptions of unconditioned ("enlightened" i.e. exploded) consciousness in the mystic traditions. As soon as the first imprint is made, structure emerges out of the creative void. The growing mind, alas, becomes trapped within this structure. It identifies with the structure; in a sense, it *becomes* the structure.

This entire process is analyzed in G. Spencer Brown's *Laws of Form;* and Brown was writing about the foundations of mathematics and logic. But every sensitive reader knows that Brown is also talking about a process we have all passed through in creating, out of an infinite ocean of signals, those particular constructs we call "myself" and "my world." Not surprisingly, many acid-heads have said that Brown's math is the best description ever written of an LSD trip.

Each successive imprint complicates the software which programs our experience and *which we experience as "reality."*

Conditioning and learning build further networks onto this bedrock of imprinted software. The total structure of this brain-circuitry makes up our map of the world. It is what our Thinker thinks, and our Prover mechanically fits all incoming signals to the limitations of this map.

Following Dr. Timothy Leary (with a few modifications) we shall divide this brain hardware into eight circuits *for convenience.* ("For convenience" means that this is the best map I know at present. I assume it will be replaced by a better map within 10 or 15 years; and in any case, the map is not the territory.)

Four of the circuits are "antique" and conservative, they exist in everybody (except feral children).

1. *The Oral Bio-Survival Circuit.* This is imprinted by the mother or the first mothering object and conditioned by subsequent nourishment or threat. It is primarily concerned with sucking, feeding, cuddling, and body security. It retreats mechanically from the noxious or predatory -- or from anything *associated* (by imprinting or conditioning) with the noxious or predatory.

2. *The Anal Emotional-Territorial Circuit.* This is imprinted in the "Toddling" stage when the infant rises up, walks about and begins to struggle for power within the family structure. This mostly mammalian circuit processes territorial rules, emotional

games, or cons, pecking order and rituals of *domination* or *submission.*

3. *The Time-Binding Semantic Circuit.* This is imprinted and conditioned by human artifacts and symbol systems. It "handles" and "packages" the environment, classifying everything according to the local reality tunnel. Invention, calculation, prediction and transmitting signals across generations are its functions.

4. *The "Moral" Socio-Sexual Circuit.* This is imprinted by the first orgasm-mating experiences at puberty and is conditioned by tribal taboos. It processes sexual pleasure, local definitions of "right" and "wrong," reproduction, adult-parental personality (sex role) and nurture of the young.

The development of these circuits as the brain evolved through evolution, and as each domesticated primate (human) brain recapitulates evolution in growing from infancy to adulthood, makes possible gene-pool survival, mammalian sociobiology (pecking order, or politics) and transmission of culture.

The second group of four brain circuits is much newer, and each circuit exists at present only in minorities. Where the antique circuits recapitulate evolution-to-the-present, these futuristic circuits *pre*capitulate our future evolution.

5. *The Holistic Neurosomatic Circuit.* This is imprinted by *ecstatic experience,* via biological or chemical yogas. It processes neurosomatic ("mind-body") feedback loops, somatic-sensory bliss, feeling "high," "faith-healing," etc. Christian Science and holistic medicine consist of tricks or gimmicks to get this circuit into action at least temporarily; Tantra yoga is concerned with shifting consciousness entirely into this circuit.

6. *The Collective Neurogenetic Circuit.* This is imprinted by advanced yogas (bio-chemical-electrical stresses). It processes DNA-RNA- brain feedback systems and is "collective" in that it contains and has access to the whole evolutionary "script," past and future. Experience of this circuit is numinous, "mystical," mind-shattering; here dwell the archetypes of Jung's Collective Unconscious -- Gods, Goddesses, Demons, Hairy Dwarfs and other personifications of the DNA programs (instincts) that govern us.

7. *The Metaprogramming Circuit.* This is imprinted by very advanced yogas. It consists, in modern terms, of cybernetic consciousness, reprogramming and reimprinting all other circuits,

even reprogramming itself, making possible conscious choice between alternative universes or reality tunnels.

8. *The Non-Local Quantum Circuit.* This is imprinted by Shock, by "near-death" or "clincal death" experience, by OOBEs (out-of-body-experiences), by trans-time perceptions ("precognition"), by trans-space visions (ESP), etc. It tunes the brain into the non-local quantum communication system suggested by physicists such as Bohm, Walker, Sarfatti, Bell, etc.

These circuits will be explained in detail as we proceed.

EXERCIZES

1. Go to a home-computer shop and get a demonstration of how a computer works. Then re-read this chapter.

2. If you can afford it -- and you will be able to afford it soon because prices are dropping rapidly in this area -- *buy* a home computer.

3. To understand *hardware* and *software* (as applied to the human brain) perform the following meditation.

Sit in a room where you will not be disturbed for a half hour and begin thinking, "I am sitting in this room doing this exercize because . . ." and list as many of the "causes" as you can think of.

For instance, you are doing this exercize because, obviously, you read about it in this book. Why did you buy this book? Did somebody recommend it? How did that person come into your life? If you just picked the book up in a store, why did you happen to be in just that store on just that day?

Why do you read books of this sort -- on psychology, consciousness, evolution etc.? How did you get interested in those fields? Who turned you on, and how long ago? What factors in your childhood inclined you to be interested in these subjects later?

Why are you doing this exercize in *this* room and not elsewhere? Why did you buy or rent this house or apartment? Why are you in this city and not another? Why on this continent and not another?

Why are you here at all -- that is, how did your parents meet? Did they consciously decide to have a child, do you happen to know, or were you an accident? What cities were they born in? If in different cities, why did they move in space-time so that their paths would intersect?

Why is this planet capable of supporting life, and why did it produce the kind of life that would dream up an exercize of this sort?

Repeat this exercize a few days later, trying to ask and answer fifty questions you didn't think of the first time. *(Note that you cannot ever ask all possible questions.)*

Avoid all metaphysical speculations (e.g. karma, reincarnation, "destiny" etc.). The point of the exercize will be mind-blowing enough without introducing "occult" theories, and it will be more startling if you carefully avoid such overtly "mystical" speculations.

4. Pick up any household item -- a spoon, a pen, a cup etc. Perform the same exercize as above -- why is it here? Who invented it, if you can find out? How did the invention get to this continent? Who manufactured it? Why did they manufacture that instead of birdcages? Why did they become manufacturers instead of musicians? Why did you buy it? Why did you pick that object, of all the objects in your house, for this meditation?

ANSWER QUICKLY NOW

ARE YOU YOUR HARDWARE, OR YOUR SOFTWARE?

OR BOTH?

CHAPTER THREE

THE ORAL BIO-SURVIVAL CIRCUIT

Genes, like Leibnitz's monads, have no windows;
the higher properties of life are emergent.

Edward Wilson, Sociobiology

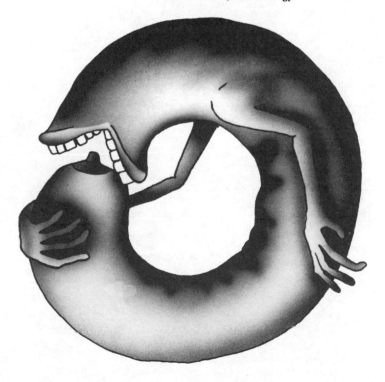

Few of our ancestors were perfect ladies or gentlemen; the majority of them were not even mammals.

Any multi-cellular organism must, if it is to survive, contain a hard-wired bio-survival circuit, which very simply programs an either-or choice: GO FORWARD to the nourishing, the protective, or GO BACK, away from the threatening, the predatory. Any mammal hooks the bio-survival circuit to the first imprinted bio-survival object: the teat. Bio-survival and orality are deeply blended in all mammals, including domesticated primates (humans). This is why, despite the Cancer Terror, an estimated 85,000,000 Americans still smoke cigarettes. Others chew gum(spearmint, juicy fruit, even sugar-free: something for every taste), bite their fingernails, gnaw their knuckles, scrunch pencil stubs, eat more than they need (Potato chips, anyone? a Mars bar maybe? pretzels, peanuts, cashews, do you want the cheese and crackers with your beer, mac? And do try the canapes, Mrs. Miller). Some chew their lips, gobble tranks and uppers, even munch their mustaches. What goes on in the bedroom is known to the Kinsey Institute and anyone who has seen a porn film.

How important is this oral imprinting? We read of a baby giraffe whose mother was accidentally killed by a jeep immediately after birth. The neonate, following hard-wired genetic programs, "imprinted" the first object that roughly fit the giraffe archetype -- the jeep itself. He followed the machine around, vocalized to it, attempted to suckle from it, and, when adult, tried to mate with it.

Similarly, Konrad Lorenz tells of a gosling who accidentally imprinted a ping-pong ball and spent his adult life, indifferent to female geese, attempting to sexually mount ping-pong balls.

As Charles Darwin noted:

In our maturer years, when an object of vision is presented to us which bears any similitude to the form of the female bosom . . .we feel a general glow of delight which seems to influence all of our senses. . . . .

The ancients pictured the great mother goddess Diana of Ephesus with literally dozens of breasts and St. Paul reports hearing her worshippers chanting rapturously "Great is Diana!" There is virtually no great artist who has not left us a portrait, or many portraits, of the nude female form, especially the breasts; and even in non-human scenes, curves are introduced wherever possible. Architects break the Euclidean straight line to introduce such curves at the slightest pretext -- arches, Moorish domes, etc. The curves of the suspension bridge are necessitated by Newton's laws ("Gravity's rainbow," in Pynchon's phrase) but, still, these double catenary curves are esthetically pleasing for the reasons Darwin suggests. As for music -- where did we first hear it, who sang or hummed to us, and against what part of her body were we held?

Mountain climbers are reduced, like Mallory, to saying "Because it's there," when trying to explain their compulsion to ascend those conic peaks.

Our eating untensils (oral gratification tools) tend to be rounded or curved. Square plates or saucers look "campy" or strange.

UFOs come in a variety of shapes, but the most popular are the oval and conic.

Freudians suggest that opiate addiction is an attempt to return to the womb. In keeping with our theory, it is more likely that opium and its derivatives return us to the "safe space" on the bio-survival circuit, the warm, snug place of bio-security; opiates may trigger neurotransmitters* characteristic of breast-feeding.

In summary: the bio-survival circuit is DNA-programmed to seek a comfort-safety zone around a mothering organism. If a mother isn't present, the closet substitute in the environment will be imprinted. For the orphan giraffe, a *four-wheeled* jeep was chosen to stand in for the *four-legged* mother. The gosling who could not find the *round,* white body of the mother-goose fixated a *round,* white ping-pong ball.

The "wiring" of this circuit, in primitive form, occurred in the first organisms, between three and four billion years ago. In the modern human, this structure remains in the *brain stem* and in the *autonomic ("involuntary") nervous system,* where it is inter-

---

*Neurotransmitters are chemicals which alter the electro-colloidal balance of the brain and hence change the perceptual field. Brain-change agents.

connected with the endocrine and other life-support systems. This is why disturbances on this circuit act "all over the body at once" and generally *take the form of physical symptoms rather than "mental" symptoms and usually get referred to the M.D. instead of the psychiatrist.*

It must be stressed that we are still in a primitive stage of evolution and conditions on this planet are quite brutal. Radical pediatricians insist, with good evidence, that childbirth by conventional means in a conventional hospital is almost always traumatic for the newborn -- creates a bad imprint, in our language. Our child-rearing methods are far from ideal also, adding bad conditioning on top of bad imprinting. And the general violence of our societies to date -- including wars, revolutions, civil wars and the "undeclared civil war" of the predatory criminal class in every "civilized" nation -- keeps the first circuit of most people in an emergency state far too much of the time.

In 1968, a U.S. Public Health survey showed that 85% of the population had one or more symptoms that we would call bad first circuit imprinting or conditioning. These symptoms included dizzy spells, heart palpitations, wet palms and frequent nightmares.

This means that 85 out of the next 100 people you meet should be regarded as, more or less, "the Walking Wounded."

This is the first level of meaning in our brutal, cynical proposition that most people are almost as mechanical as sci-fi robots. A man or woman entering a new situation with the anxiety chemicals* of a frightened infant coursing through the brain stem is not going to be able to *observe, judge* or *decide* anything very accurately.

And this is why Gurdjieff said, in his own jargon, that people are asleep and having nightmares.

"FAIRNESS? DECENCY? HOW CAN YOU EXPECT FAIRNESS OR DECENCY ON A PLANET OF SLEEPING PEOPLE?" G. I. Gurdjieff

---

*We specially refer to adrenalin and adrenalutin, which signal the whole organism to prepare to fight or flee.

This was the viewpoint of the earliest Christians, later condemned as heretics (Gnostics) by the Roman bureaucrats. The *Gospel of Truth,* first century, says bluntly that history is a nightmare:

> . . .as if (mankind) were sunk in sleep and found themselves in disturbing dreams. Either (there is) a place to which they are fleeing . . . or they are involved in striking blows, or they are receiving blows themselves . . . sometimes it is as if people were murdering them . . . or they themselves are killing their neighbors . . .

To these first Christians, as to the Buddhists, *awakening* literally meant coming out of this nightmare of terrifying fantasies. In our terminology, it means correcting the imprints that cause us to behave and perceive like very badly (inappropriately) wired robots and suddenly seeing the real world.

It must be emphasized that this circuit, being the oldest in evolutionary development, is the most mechanical, and the most *rapid.* One is not conscious of time at all on the bio-survival circuit. Observe the speed of your dog's reaction at the first sound of an intruder: the threatening bark, and the movement of the whole body to alert status, is *automatic.* Then the dog starts taking in other cues, to determine how this particular intruder should be treated.

As Robert Ardrey reports the remarks of primatologist Ray Carpenter, to understand this part of your brain . . .

> Imagine that you are a monkey and you're running along a path past a rock and unexpectedly meet face to face another animal. Now, before you know whether to attack it, to flee it, or to ignore it, you must make a series of decisions. Is it monkey or non-monkey? If non-monkey, is it pro-monkey or anti-monkey? If monkey, is it male or female? If female, is she interested? If male, is it adult or juvenile? If adult, is it of my group or some other? . . . You have about one fifth of a second to make all these decisions, or you could be attacked.

The bio-survival program first attaches to the safe space around the mother (oral imprint), and then with age moves further and further out, exploring what is safe and what is not. Without hard-wired genetic programs (i.e. *automatic* programs) this second stage would be impossible, and no mammal would ever leave the teat. The hard-wired programs act automatically "*UNCONSCIOUSLY*" because if you had to stop and think out each situation, you would be eaten by the first predator.

Of course, the imprint is made by *chance* -- by the circumstances at the moment of imprint vulnerability. (Recall the gosling who imprinted the ping-pong ball.) Some imprint bravery, inquisitiveness and the exploratory drive; others imprint timidity, neophobia (fear of novelty) and withdrawal, of which the extreme case is the sad imprint called *autism* or childhood schizophrenia.

All of which is robotic, *until* one learns how to reprogram and reimprint one's own brain circuits. In most cases, such meta-programming skill is never acquired. It all goes by in a flash, on mechanical auto-pilot, in *zero* time. "I just found myself doing it," says the soldier as he is being court-martialled for cowardice or decorated for bravery.

It's safe out here!

TIMID RETREAT

CONFIDENT ADVANCE

Oh, Mommy, take me home!

First circuit bio-survival consciousness is "one-dimensional"

Of course, on top of the hard-wired imprinting of the bio-survival circuit comes "softer" conditioning. This allows the safe-space perimeter to be generalized outward from the mother's body to the pack or tribe -- the "extended family."

Every social animal has, in addition to the Darwinian "instinct" (genetic program) of self-preservation, a similar "instinct" to protect the gene-pool. This is the basis of altruism, and social animals could not survive without it.

Wild dogs (and wolves) bark to warn the rest of the pack that an intruder is coming. Your domesticated dog identifies you as a pack-leader; he barks to warn you that an intruder is coming. (He also barks, of course, to warn the intruder that he is ready to fight for his territory.)

As civilization has advanced, the pack-bond (the tribe, the extended family) *has been broken.* This is the root of the widely-diagnosed *"anomie"* or "alienation" or "existential anguish" about which so many social critics have written so eloquently. What has happened is that the conditioning of the bio-survival bond to the gene-pool has been replaced by *a conditioning of bio-survival drives to hook onto the peculiar tickets which we call "money".*

Concretely, a modern man or woman doesn't look for bio-survival security in the gene-pool, the pack, the extended family. Bio-survival depends on getting the tickets. "You can't *live* without money," as the Living Theatre troop used to cry out in anguish. If the tickets are withdrawn, acute bio-survival anxiety appears at once.

Imagine, as vividly as possible, what you would feel, and what you would do, if all your sources to bio-survival tickets (money) were cut off tomorrow. This is precisely what tribal men and women feel if cut off from the tribe; it is why exile, or even ostracism, were sufficient punishments to enforce tribal conformity throughout most of human history. As recently as Shakespeare's day the threat of exile was an acute terror signal ("Banished!" cries Romeo, "the damned use that word in Hell!")

In traditional society, belonging to the tribe was bio-security; exile was terror, and real threat of death. In modern society, having the tickets (money) is bio-security; having the tickets withdrawn is terror.

Welfare-ism, socialism, totalitarianism, etc. represent attempts, in varying degrees of rationality and hysteria, to re-create the tribal bond by making the State stand-in for the gene-pool. Conservatives who claim that no form of Welfare is tolerable to them are asking that people live with total bio-survival anxiety *anomie* combined with terror. The conservatives, of course, vaguely recognize this and ask for "local charity" to replace State Welfare -- i.e. they ask for the gene-pool to be restored by magic, among people (denizens of a typical city) who are not genetically related at all.

On the other hand, the State is not a gene-pool or a tribe, and cannot really play the bio-survival unit convincingly. Everybody on Welfare becomes paranoid, because they are continually worrying that they are going to get cut off ("exiled") for some minor infraction of the increasingly incomprehensible bureaucratic rules. And in real totalitarianism, in which the bogus identification of the State with the tribe is carried to the point of a new mysticism, the paranoia becomes total.

Real bonding can only occur in face-to-face groups of reasonable size. Hence, the perpetual attempt (however implausible in industrial circumstances) to decentralize, to go back to the tribal ethos, to replace the State with syndicates (as in anarchism) or affinity-groups (Reich's "Consciousness III"). Recall the hippie crash-pad of the sixties, which lives on in many rural communes.

Back in the real world, the tickets called *"money"* are the bio-survival bond for most people. Anti-Semitism is a complex aberration, of many facets and causes, but in its classic form (the "Jewish Bankers' Conspiracy") it simply holds that a hostile gene-pool controls the tickets for bio-security. Such paranoia is inevitable in a money economy; junkies have similar myths about who controls the supply of heroin. Thus, as anti-Semitism has declined in America, the "Bankers' Conspiracy" lives on in a new form. Now the villains are old New England WASP families, the "Yankee Establishment." Some Leftists will even show you charts of the genealogies of these WASP bankers, the way anti-Semites used to show Rothschild genealogies.

THE ALPHA MALES EAT FIRST: THE RUNTS OF THE LITTER GET WHATEVER IS LEFT OVER.

C.H. Douglas, the engineer and economist, once made up a chart, which he showed to the MacMillan Commission in 1932 when they were discussing money and credit regulation. The chart graphed the rise and fall of interest rates from the defeat of Napoleon in 1812 to the date the Commission met in 1932, and on the same scale, the rise and fall of the suicide rate in that 120-year period.

The two curves were virtually identical. Every time the interest rate went up, so did the suicide rate; when interest went down, so did suicide. This can hardly be "coincidence." When interest rises, a certain number of businessmen go bankrupt, a certain number of workers are thrown out of their jobs, and everybody's bio-survival anxiety generally increases.

Marxists and other radicals are urgently aware of such factors in "mental health" and hence scornful of all types of academic psychology which ignore these bio-survival issues. Unfortunately, the Marxist remedy -- making everybody dependent for bio-survival on the whims of a State bureaucracy -- is a cure worse than the disease.

Bio-survival anxiety will only permanently disappear when world-wide wealth has reached a level, and a distribution, where, without totalitarianism, everyone has enough *tickets*.

The Hunger Project, the idea of the Guaranteed Annual Income etc. represent groping toward that goal. The ideal can only be achieved in a technology of abundance.

Extreme cases -- persons who take their *heaviest* imprint on the first (oral) circuit -- tend to be viscerotonic, because this imprint determines lifelong endocrine and glandular processes. Thus, in extreme they are "baby-faced" in adult life, never lose their "baby-fat," are plump and round and gentle, etc. They are easily "hurt" (threatened: terrified) by disapproval of any sort, because in the baby-circuit of the brain, *disapproval* suggests *extinction* by loss of the food supply.

We all have this circuit and need to exercize it periodically. Cuddling, sucking, hugging etc. and daily playing with (a) one's own body (b) another's body and (c) the environment, are perpetually necessary to neurosomatic-endocrine health. Those who deny such primordial functions because of rigid imprinting on the Third (rationalistic) or Fourth (moralistic) circuit tend to become "dried up," "prune-faced," unattractive, "cold," and muscularly rigid.

The baby-functions of playing with one's own body, another's body and the environment continue throughout life in all animals. This "playfulness" is a marked characteristic of all conspicuously healthy individuals of the sort Maslow calls "self-actualizers."

If this initial imprint is negative -- if the universe in general and other humans in particular are imprinted as dangerous, hostile and frightening -- the Prover will go on throughout life adjusting all perceptions to fit this map. This is what is known as the "Injustice Collector" syndrome (in the language of Dr. Edmund Bergler).

Such a pattern is unconscious in three ways. It is unconscious because automatic: it happens without thought, as a robot program. It is also unconscious because it began before the infant had language and hence it is pre-verbal, inarticulate, *felt* rather than considered. And it is unconscious because it is all-over-the-body-at-once. Specifically, it is characterized by the *Respiratory Block* first noted by Wilhelm Reich: a chronic muscular armoring that prevents proper, relaxed breathing. Popular speech recognizes this state as "being up-tight."

All of the most successful re-imprinting techniques (therapies) for this kind of chronic anxiety work on the body first, not on the "mind." The Reichians, Rolfers, Primal Scream therapists, Orr's "rebirthers," Gestaltists etc. all know, whatever specialized jargons they may use, that a bad bio-survival imprint can only be corrected by working on the biological being itself, the body that feels perpetually vulnerable and under attack.

As Gregory Bateson has pointed out, Konrad Lorenz acquired his marvelous insights into the imprinting process -- for which he won the Nobel prize -- by consciously imitating the body-movements of the animals he was studying. Watching Lorenz lecture, one could "see" each animal he discussed, because Lorenz would dramatize or "become" that animal, in the manner of a Method Actor.

Even earlier, Wilhelm Reich discovered that he could understand his patients with remarkable clarity by imitating their characteristic body movements and postures. The bio-survival imprints, especially traumatic ones, are all-over-the-body, *frozen* (in Reich's metaphor) in chronic muscle and gland mechanisms.

If you can't understand somebody's "irrational" behavior, start by observing their breathing. You will very quickly get an idea of what is bothering them. This is why all schools of yoga Buddhist, Hindu or Sufi -- place such emphasis on restoring natural breathing before trying to move the student on to higher circuits and wider consciousness.

This is of more than "psychological" import. Every study of the psychosomatic aspects of cancer and asthma, for instance, finds this pattern of chronic muscular contraction (subjectively felt as anxiety) among the predisposing factors. What the Thinker thinks, the Prover proves. People are strangling their inner organs every day because they are *afraid.*

Mary Baker Eddy may have been exaggerating slightly when she said "All illness is manifested fear;" but holistic medicine more and more recognizes that if that damned word "all" is replaced by a more tentative "most," Mrs. Eddy was close to the facts.

Even old-fangled M.D.s who won't consider holistic ideas for a minute, admit that some persons are mysteriously "more susceptible" to disease than other persons. What is this metaphysical "susceptibility"? Anthropologist Ashley Montagu has collected numerous statistics on children who were deprived of maternal love at the crucial point of imprint vulnerability in infancy. They not only died younger than the national average, but were sicklier all their lives and even grew up to be several inches shorter than the average adult height for their sex.

What makes for "susceptibility" (aside from possible genetic factors) can only be such an anxiety imprint (muscle tension) on the first circuit.

Christian Science -- or any other religion that dogmatically insists that *"God" wants us to be happy and successful* -- can cure such conditions "miraculously." *What the Thinker thinks, the Prover proves.* Absolute faith that "God" is supporting you, beamed out from the brain all day long, day after day, signals the muscles to relax, and natural buoyancy and health returns.

Throughout human life, when the bio-survival circuit senses danger, all other mental activity ceases. All other circuits shut down until the bio-survival problem is "solved," realistically or symbolically. This is of crucial importance in mind-washing and brain-programming.

To create a new imprint, first reduce the subject to the state of infancy, i.e. bio-survival vulnerability. We will enlarge upon this later.

In pre-neurological terms, the bio-survival circuit is what we usually call "consciousness," *per se.* It is the sense of being here-now, in this vulnerable body, subject to the raw energies and forces of the physical universe. When we are "unconscious," the bio-survival circuit is turned off and doctors may cut us up without our attempting to flee or even cry out.

EXERCIZES

1. Determine to *enjoy* this primitive circuit fully from now on. Play with yourself and others and the environment *shamelessly,* like a newborn baby. Meditate on "Unless ye become as a little child, ye shall in no wise enter the Kingdom of Heaven."

2. Never mind your diet -- you will reach the optimum weight for your height when your brain is operating properly. Enjoy *one* really sweet and gooey desert every week.

3. Get "high" (on marijuana if this is permissible to your superego, or on ginseng, which is legal everywhere and recommended by many holistic physicians) and then go to a health spa. Enjoy a good swim, a massage and a sauna. Repeat every week, forever.

4. Take a course on *kung fu* or *karate* for at least three months, then re-read this whole chapter. You will be surprised at how much more *every* sentence will mean.

5. Lie on your back and pant rapidly to the count of 20. (Each exhale-inhale cycle counts as one, not as two.) Panting means breathing rapidly through your mouth, as forbidden by almost all experts on health, but this is only an exercise, not a full-time practise. When you reach 20, stop and resume nose-breathing, in the slow, rhythmic manner recommended by yogis, to the count of 20. Then repeat the panting to the count of 20. Then repeat proper yoga breathing.

This is known as the "breath of fire" in Tantric yoga. The results are most amusing and enlightening. Try it!*

6. Visit an aquarium and *observe very closely*. Try to see the bio-survival circuit of the fish brain in operation and recognize when and how that circuit in your own brain has operated throughout your life.

7. If you don't have a baby, or haven't had one for many years, play with somebody else's baby for an hour. Then re-read this chapter.

*Like opiate use, this exercize seems to trigger neuro-transmitters similar to mother's milk, i.e. it takes you back to the snug security of breast-feeding. And it is not addictive.

CHAPTER FOUR

THE ANAL EMOTIONAL TERRITORIAL CIRCUIT

Run, puppy, run!
Run, puppy, run!
Yonder comes the big dog ---
Run, puppy, run!

Children's rhyme

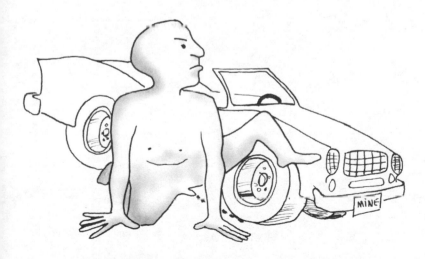

The second circuit, the emotional-territorial networks of the brain, is concerned entirely with power politics. This "patriotic" circuit is built into all vertebrates and is perhaps 500 million to 1000 million years old. In the modern human it seems to be centralized in the *thalamus* -- the "back brain" or "old brain"and is linked with the *voluntary nervous system* and the *muscles.*

This circuit appears in each newborn when the DNA master tape sends out RNA messenger molecules to trigger the mutation from neonate to *"toddler,"* which involves first of all standing erect. Walking, mastering gravity, overcoming physical obstacles and learning to manipulate others politically are the vulnerable points at which imprinting and heavy conditioning occur. The muscles that perform these power functions are quickly programmed with what become chronic, life-long reflexes.

Depending as always on the accidents of the environment, what happens at points of neurological vulnerability — this circuit will organize itself into a strong, dominating role in the pack (or family) or a weak, submissive role. Without going into the jungles with the ethologists, one can observe this mammalian imprinting process in any litter of puppies. It is very quickly determined who is TOP DOG and who is BOTTOM DOG.

Status in the pack or tribe is assigned on the basis of pre-verbal signalling system (kinesics) in which these muscle reflexes are crucial. All of the emotional *games* or *cons* listed in the popular psycholgical game-manuals of Dr. Eric Berne and the Transactional Analysts are second circuit imprints, or standard mammalian politics.

To quote from my novel *Schrödinger's Cat:*

Most of the domesticated primates of Terra did not know they were primates. They thought they were something apart from and "superior" to the rest of the planet.

Even Benny Benedict's "One Month to Go" column was based on that illusion. Benny had actually read Darwin once, in college a long time ago, and had heard of sciences like ethology and ecology, but the facts of evolution had never really registered on him. He never thought of himself as a primate. He never realized his friends and associates were primates. Above all, he never understood that the *alpha males* of Unistat were typical leaders of primate bands. As a result of this inability to see the obvious, Benny was constantly alarmed and terrified by the behavior of himself, his friends and associates and especially the alpha males of the pack. Since he didn't know it was ordinary primate behavior, it seemed just awful to him.

Since a great deal of primate behavior was considered just awful, most of the domesticated primates spent most of their time trying to conceal what they were doing.

Some of the primates got caught by other primates. All of the primates lived in dread of getting caught.

Those who got caught were called no-good shits.

The term no-good shit was a deep expression of primate psychology. For instance, one wild primate (a chimpanzee) taught sign language by two domesticated primates (scientists) spontaneously put together the signs for "shit" and "scientist" to describe a scientist she didn't like. She was calling him shit-scientist. She also put together the signs for "shit" and "chimpanzee" for another chimpanzee she didn't like. She was calling him shit-chimpanzee.

"You no-good shit," domesticate primates often said to each other.

This metaphor was deep in primate psychology because primates mark their territories with excretions, and sometimes they threw excretions at each other when disputing over territories.

One primate wrote a long book describing in vivid detail how his political enemies should be punished. He imagined them in an enormous hole in the ground, with flames and smoke and rivers of shit. This primate was named Dante Alighieri.

Another primate wrote that every primate infant goes through a stage of being chiefly concerned with bio-survival, i.e. food, i.e. Mommie's Titty. He called this the Oral Stage. He said the infant next went on to a stage of learning mammalian politics, i.e. recognizing the Father (alpha-male) and his Authority and territorial demands. He called this, with an insight that few primates shared, the Anal Stage.

This primate was named Freud. He had taken his own nervous system apart and examined its component circuits by periodically altering its structure with neurochemicals.

Among the anal insults exchanged by domesticated primates when fighting for their space were: "Up your ass," "Go shit in your hat," "You're full of shit," and many others.

One of the most admired alpha-males in the Kingdom of the Franks was General Canbronne. General Canbronne won this adulation for the answer he once gave when asked to surrender.

"Merde," was the answer General Canbronne gave.

The word petard means a kind of bomb. It comes from the same Olde English root as fart.

General Canbronne's mentality was typical of the alpha-males of the military caste.

When primates went to war or got violent in other ways, they always said they were about to knock the shit out of the enemy.

They also spoke of dumping on each other.

"NATIONALISM"

The standard "authority" reflex on the emotional-territorial circuit is to swell the muscles and howl. You will find this among birds as well as mammals, and in the Board meeting of your local bank. The standard "submission" reflex is to shrink the muscles, lower the head, and "crawl away." You will find this among dogs, primates, fowl and employees who wish to keep their jobs everywhere.

If the first (bio-survival) circuit is chiefly imprinted by the mother, the second (emotional-territorial) circuit is chiefly imprinted by the father -- the nearest *alpha male*. It has been proposed, by sociologist G. Rattray Taylor that societies swing back and forth between "Matrist" periods, in which motherly oral values predominate, and "Patrist" periods, in which fatherly anal values are in ascendance.

THE STANDARD AUTHORITY REFLEX

Taylor's table of the characteristics of these "Matrist" and "Patrist" periods is as follows:

MATRIST	PATRIST
Permissive toward sex	Restrictive toward sex
Freedom for women	Limitation of freedom for women
Women have high status	Women have low status
Chastity not valued	Chastity highly valued
Egalitarian	Authoritarian
Progressive	Conservative
No distrust of research	Distrust of Research
Spontaneous	Inhibitions
Sex differences minimized	Sex differences maximized
Fear of incest	Fear of homosexuality
Hedonic	Ascetic
Mother Goddess	Father God

Whether or not societies wobble between these extremes as Taylor claims, individuals certainly do. These are merely the consequences of (a) having the heaviest imprint on the oral (Matrist) bio-survival circuit or (b) having the heaviest imprint on the anal (Patrist) territorial circuit.

In pre-ethological terms, the emotional-territorial circuit is what we usually call "ego." *Ego is simply the mammalian recognition of one's status in the pack;* it is a "role" as sociologists say, a single brain circuit which mistakes itself for the whole Self, the entire brain-mind apparatus. The "egotist" behaves like "a two year old," in the common saying, because Ego is the imprint of the toddling and toilet-training stage.

The question of how human an animal is (especially a pet dog or cat) never ceases to divide scientists from laypersons -- and one scientist from another. In terms of the present theory, the differences between domesticated primates (humans) and other domesticated animals are virtually nil, as long as we are talking *only* about the first two circuits. (Since most people spend most of their time on these primitive circuits, the differences are often much less obvious than the similarities.) Real differences begin to appear when the third, semantic circuit enters the picture.

For instance, novice dog-trainers always make the mistake of

MOST MAMMALS MARK THEIR TERRITORIES WITH EXCRETIONS. DOMESTICATED PRIMATES MARK THEIR TERRITORIES WITH INK EXCRETIONS ON PAPER.

using *too many words*. Because the dog is so "human" in so many ways (canines, like primates, are great mimics), the novice imputes too much "humanity" to them. The average dog has a vocabulary of around 150 words, and within that semantic universe is quite bright. It is very easy to teach a dog the meaning of "Sit," "Stay," "Attack," etc.; and the dog will learn the meaning of "walk" and "food" even without your trying to teach him. The problem begins when the novice expects the dog to understand something like "No, no, Fritz -- anywhere else in the bedroom, but not on the bed." Even a non-English-speaking human would not grasp that, except vaguely. The dog gives up on such sentences and guesses what he can from your mammalian (and unconscious) *body-language*.

Understanding these distinctions can vastly improve primate-canine communication. For instance, my wife, a sociologist, trained one dog not to beg at the table in the most direct mammalian language possible. She simply *growled* at him the first few times he approached her while she was eating. (She had been reading ethology, of course.) The dog understood fully; he soon learned to avoid the table while the Pack-Leaders (my wife and myself) were eating. His genetic programs told him we were the Big Dogs, or as close to the Big Dogs as he could find in that environment; dogs, like wolves, have a genetic program about not annoying the Big Dogs while they're eating. The growl told him all he needed to know about the local parameters of that rule.

Persons (extreme cases) who take the *heaviest* imprint on this territorial-emotional circuit tend to be musculotonic. That is, they hold most of their attention and energy in the muscular attack-defense systems and grow up medium weight -- *heavy* enough to be hard to knock down, *light* enough to be quick and sinewy. Often, they become body-builders, weight-lifters etc. and have an extraordinary absorption in demonstrating their strength. (Even shaking hands with them, you get the message that they are not exchanging amity but demonstrating power.)

Most societies shunt these types into the military where their propensities are put to proper ethological use, defending the tribal turf. The anal orientation of this circuit explains the oddity of military speech first noted by Norman Mailer: "ass" means one's whole self and "shit" means all surrounding circumstance.

Viscerotonic

EXTREME
Circuit I Type
Oral Imprint

Musculotonic

EXTREME
Circuit II Type
Anal Imprint

IMPRINTING EFFECTS THE WHOLE NERVOUS SYSTEM. THE NERVOUS SYSTEM EFFECTS THE WHOLE BODY.

47

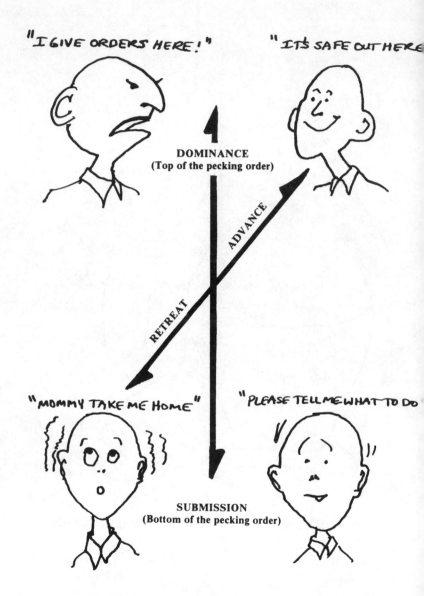

The second, emotional-territorial circuit creates a two-dimensional social space in conjunction with first-circuit advance-retreat.

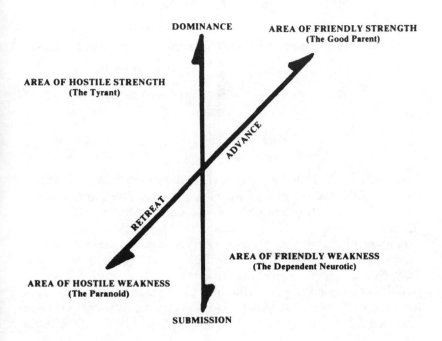

The grid of Circuits I and II creates four quadrants. Note that Hostile Strength (the tyrant) is inclined to paranoid withdrawal; he must govern, but he is also afraid. Of the careers of Hitler, Stalin, Howard Hughes etc. and the inaccessible Castle and Court in Kafka's allegories. Note also that the dependent neurotic is not in retreat at all; he or she advances upon you, demanding fulfillment of emotional "needs" (imprints).

These four quadrants have been known since the dawn of self-consciousness. For instance, in the terminology of the medieval psychology of "humours," these four imprint-types are known as:

CHOLERIC HUMOR	**PHLEGMATIC HUMOR**
(Hostile Strength)	(Friendly Strength)
BILIOUS HUMOR	**MELANCHOLY HUMOR**
(Hostile Weakness)	(Friendly) Weakness)

Clockwise, the Phlegmatic type (friendly strength) was identified with the *Lion* archetype and the element, *fire*. The Lion, because of the dignity of these big cats, represents "good" strength, and the fire represents power. The Melancholic type (friendly weakness) was identified with the *Angel* archetype and the element *water*: these people are "too sensitive to fight" and "go with the flow." The Bilious types were identified with the *Bull* archetype (truculent suspicion, paranoia) and the element, *earth*, standing for sluggish pseudo "stupidity." (This is the traditional stance of defeated races dealing with their conquerors.) The Choleric types (hostile strength) were identified with the *Eagle* archetype (symbol of Imperial Rome, the German royal family etc.) and the element *air;* air probably means sky, because these types seem "high and mighty."

These symbols go back a long way; Cabalists find them in the Old Testament (where, indeed, the lion-angel-bull-eagle appear in Ezekiel). They are found constantly in Catholic art, associated with the four evangelists (Matthew-angel, Mark-lion, Luke-bull, John-eagle)* and run all through the design of Tarot card decks, medieval and modern.

*These are the Four Old Men in *Finnegans Wake,* Matt Gregory, because his last name contains *ego* equals the angel; Marcus Lyons equals the lion; Luke Tarpey equals taur, the bull; Johnny McDougal equals ougal the eagle.

In the clever language of the fashionable Transactional Analysis system, these four imprint types are categorized as the four basic life scripts, to wit:

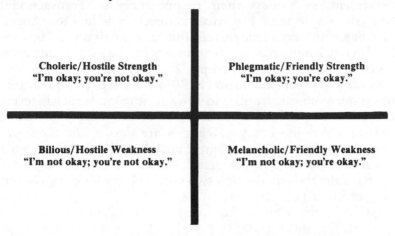

Choleric/Hostile Strength "I'm okay; you're not okay."	**Phlegmatic/Friendly Strength** "I'm okay; you're okay."
Bilious/Hostile Weakness "I'm not okay; you're not okay."	**Melancholic/Friendly Weakness** "I'm not okay; you're okay."

It is the Melancholic (friendly weakness; dependent neurotic) type who generally turn up in the psychotherapist's office seeking reimprinting voluntarily. They are not-okay, but they have great faith that the therapist is okay.

The Choleric (hostile strength) and Bilious (hostile weakness) arrive in therapy, if at all, only because their associates or families, or more commonly, a law court, has *ordered* them to try to reimprint their compulsive hostilities.

The Phlegmatic (friendly strength) type virtually never comes for psychotherapy. He or she is satisfied with his or her life, and so is the rest of society. Alas, they nonetheless can get to the position where they need therapy of some sort, simply because they may take on *too much* responsibility and carry *too many* burdens. They will generally arrive at the therapists only if sent there by an M.D. who has intuited where their ulcers came from.

This system is not meant to be rigid or to imply that there are *only* four types of humanoid robots. The later circuits, still to be discussed, modify all this considerably: some imprints are wobbly (cover two or more quadrants partly); and we are all capable of sudden brain change. It is also important to realize that the four archetypes are *for convenience only* -- and they are convenient, as witness their reappearance in Transactional Analysis, where their historical connection with Lion-Angel-Bull-Eagle isn't even recognized. But each quadrant can be subdivided much more sharply, if necessary for diagnostic purposes.

For instance, a widely used psychological test in this country the Leary Interpersonal Grid (1957) divides the four quadrants into sixteen sub-quadrants and allows one to grade each in terms of moderate-to-excessive tendency to behave that way. In the grid on which the Leary categories are drawn, the *moderate imprints* are in toward the center and the *excessive or extreme cases* are out toward the perimeter, but what is being measured is still basically the way the first two circuits (oral-bio-survival and anal-territorial) are imprinted.

To clarify this a bit further, imagine that four babies were all born at the same instant in John J. Boscowitz Memorial Hospital, Enny Town, planet Earth. We come back twenty years later and we find that each of them has a separate personality and life-style (a problem for the astrologers, but let that pass). To make things easier for us, they have actually landed in our four quadrants.

Subject #1 is Responsible/Over-Conventional (Phlegmatic). Everybody agrees that SHe (she or he) is usually a beloved community leader -- helpful, considerate, friendly and solidly successful. Some may even say SHe spoils people with kindness, forgives anything, agrees with everybody and actually enjoys governing those who cannot govern themselves. The noble Lion.

This person may be (and probably is) a total robot. That is, if SHe can *never* give orders in a strict way, is *never* able to doubt others, is *never* ego-centered, etc. then SHe has mechanically imprinted the First Quadrant, "friendly strength." On the other hand, if SHe is able to move out of the First Quadrant in appropriate situations (exercizing hostility against the marauder or predator, admitting weakness when overwhelmed). SHe has an imprinted-conditioned predilection for "I'm okay, you're okay," but is not totally -- robotized by it.

Subject #2 has, after the same twenty years of imprinting and conditioning, landed in Quadrant 2 *friendly weakness* (melacholy). SHe is self-critical, shy, timid, easily led, "spineless," and

LEARY'S GRID

THE FOUR QUADRANTS HAVE BEEN RECOGNIZED IN MANY AGES AND EXPRESSED IN MANY SYMBOLS.

always looking for somebody to Take Charge and Give Orders. The unearthly Angel, or in modern symbolism, the Flower Child.

Again, this imprinting-conditioning may be totally robotic, or there may be enough flexibility for the person to jump to another quadrant when necessary.

Subject #3 had landed, with total robothood or with some small flexibility, in Quadrant 3, "Hostile Weakness" (Bilious). SHe distrusts everybody, rebels against everything, speaks constantly in sarcasms, complains chronically and is generally bitter, resentful and (to some extent) paranoid. The sullen Bull.

Subject #4 has landed in Quadrant 4, "Hostile Strength" (Choleric), and is regarded as "bossy," cold, unfeeling, dictatorial, self-important, boastful etc. but still in the judgement of most, "a good leader." The imperial Eagle.

The irony and the tragedy of human life is that none of these subjects are aware at all of their robotry. Each will explain to you, at great length and with great conviction, why each of these robotic, endlessly repeated reflexes are *caused* by the situations around them, i.e. by the "bad" behavior of other people.

WHAT THE THINKER THINKS, THE PROVER PROVES.

Thus, if you put these four primates on a desert island, you can predict, with virtually as much certainty as a chemist telling us what will happen if four elements are compounded, that Subject #1 and #4 (Friendly Strength and Hostile Strength) will both try to take over --#1 to help the others, #4 because SHe can't imagine anybody else in control. #1 will submit to #4 because #1 wants things to run smoothly for the good of all, and they never will run smoothly if #4 is not TOP DOG. #2, Friendly Weakness, will not care whether #1 or #4 rules, just so long as somebody else is making the decisions. And #3 will complain (and complain, and complain), no matter who is in charge, while skillfully avoiding any action that would require taking personal responsibility.

The same political decisions would be made by four chimpanzees or four dogs, if they have the four imprint quadrants equally divided as in our hypothetical example.

Sociobiologists, who are very aware of these four quadrants in both human and animal societies, claim that each organism is born with a genetic predispostion to play one of these roles. Critics of sociobiology, who are dogmatic Liberals, denounce this idea as monstrous. We will not attempt to decide that difficult question here, since any attempt to decide what aspects of behavior are genetic and what are learned after birth always decends into ideological metaphysics in the prevailing absence of real data. We say merely that, whether or not you or I were born with a predispostion for one quadrant, all organisms are born with a predisposition for *imprint vulnerability,* and the imprint, once set in the neural circuitry, acts as robotically as any genetic hard-wiring.

How imprints can be changed will be discussed as we proceed. The exercizes in each chapter are intended to make imprints a little less rigid, a little more flexible.

The top two quadrants of the Leary grid -- Friendly Strength and Hostile Strength -- correspond roughly to what Nietzsche called *Herrenmoral,* the ethics of ruling classes. Indeed, "Choleric" Hostile Strength is the embodiment of Nietzsche's "Blond Beast," the primitive conqueror-pirate type we find at the dawn of every civilization. This is what Nietzsche also called the "animal" or *"unsublimated"* form of the Will to Power.

(Friendly Strength on the other hand does *not* correspond, except very slightly, to Nietzsche's *"sublimated* Will to Power." To find that we will have to wait until we come to the Fifth [Neurosomatic] Circuit -- the stage of Conscious Evolution.)

The bottom two quadrants -- Friendly Weakness and Hostile Weakness -- correspond to Nietzsche's *Sklavmoral,* the ethics of slaves, serfs and "lower"-caste or "lower"-class persons everywhere. Nietzsche's concept of *"resentiment"* -- the hidden revenge motive within "altruistic" philosophies -- claims there is an element of hostility within even the Friendly Weakness side of the grid; i.e. in conventional "Christian ethics," as typified by the image of "gentle Jesus, meek and mild." This paradox -- the Friendly Weakling is a Hostile Weakling in disguise, the Flower Child a potential Mansonized robot-killer -- reappears in modern clinical parlance as the concept of "passive aggressive." Occultists in their strange jargon describe these types as *"psychic vampires."*

This is why Nietzsche claimed that St. Paul had destroyed the *evangel* (good news) of Jesus and replaced it with a *dysangel* (bad news). The *evangel* of Jesus, as Nietzche saw it, was the *sublimated*

Will to Power, the path of conscious evolution to Superhumanity. The *dysangel,* the bad news, created by St. Paul was traditional *Sklavmoral* -- "Slaves, obey your masters," but nourish your *resentiment* with the firm belief that you are "good," and they are "evil," and you will eventually have the pleasure of watching them burn in hell forever. In Nietzsche's analysis, all Marx added to this was the idea of burning and punishing the Master Class here and now instead of waiting for "God" to attend to the matter *post mortem.*

The same analysis appears in e.e. cummings' unforgettable couplet on the Communist intelligentsia of the 1930s:

**every kumrad is a little bit
of concentrated hate**

It is interesting, in this connection, that Nietzsche dropped "psychological" language from his books as he went along and replaced it with "physiological" language. For instance, in his later works, such as *The Anti-Christ,* the *"resentiment"* within slave-morality (conventional Christianity) is diagnosed as a physiological reaction characteristic of certain physical types. Nietzsche was on the right track, but lacking neurology he looked for the physical basis of these processes in genetics alone. Imprinting theory suggests, on the contrary, that such physiological Bottom Dog reflexes are created by specific triggers at early moments of imprint vulnerability.

But they are nonetheless all-over-the-body-at-once and hence physiological. Any Method Actor knows this and his body will swell physically if he is playing a strong character and shrink if he is playing a weakling. Rod Steiger, in particular, actually seems taller or shorter depending on whether he is playing a Top Dog or a Bottom Dog.

Remember again that all these categories are for *convenience* and that nature has not employed the sharp boundaries that we use in our models of nature. Thus, with Leary's 1957 schemata, we can further sub-divide our 4 types into 16 types with 4 degrees of each, for a total of 64 sub-types.

In the next section, to simplify what may be growing too complex, we will reduce everything again just to the inter-actions of the first two circuits.

Any system for describing human behavior should be flexible enough to be extended indefinitely, and should also still contain meaning when reduced back to its fundamentals.

Since we all contain a territorial-emotional circuit we need to exercize it daily.

Playing with children is one good exercize -- especially if you play with large groups, in which case you will have to referee mammalian territorial disputes. Swimming, jogging or whatever else appeals to you is good, to keep the muscles from feeling you are trying to starve them. Trying to "psych out" somebody else's emotional state is one of the best exercizes for this circuit, and is very educational in general. It activates the old mammal centers in the thalamus where body-language communicates emotional signals.

A good General uses this circuit to "psych out" what the enemy General is planning. A good mother uses it, vice versa, to figure out what baby's howl means in each particular case.

Advanced work with this circuit, involving some hazards in personal relations, would involve such games as learning to bully somebody if you've never been able to do that before, learning to submit docilely if you've never been able to do *that* before, and learning to express anger appropriately and letting go of it when it is no longer necessary.

It will be observed by the thoughtful or visually-oriented readers that each "extreme" type can be expressed on the Leary Grid as a very off-center pie-slice:

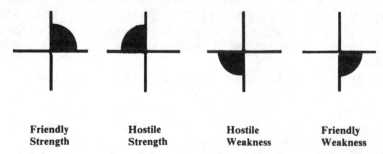

| Friendly | Hostile | Hostile | Friendly |
| Strength | Strength | Weakness | Weakness |

Obviously, an ideally "balanced" person -- that is, one not robotized and able to adjust to circumstances as they arise -- would not be so off-centered. Such a person would be able to move a little bit into each quadrant "according to the times and seasons" as the Chinese say, but would basically maintain a centered detachment between all of them. She or he could be graphed as a circle:

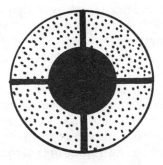

The dark inner circle would represent the adamantine individuality of this ideally detached person -- detached from robot imprints. The grey circle would represent the ability to move out into each quadrant in times when that was necessary.

Circles of this sort, called *mandalas,* are widely used for meditation in the Buddhist tradition. Often they are cornered by four demons who evidently, like the Occidental lion, bull, angel and eagle, represent the extremes to be avoided.

...being humus, the same roturns.
Joyce, Finnegans Wake

EXERCIZES

1. Whenever you meet a young male or female, ask yourself consciously, "If it came to hand-to-hand combat, could I beat him/her?" Then try to determine how much of your behavior is based on *unconsciously* asking and answering that question *via* pre-verbal "body language."

2. Get roaring drunk and pound the table, telling everybody in a loud voice just what dumb ass-holes they all are.*

3. Get a book on meditation, practise for two fifteen-minute sessions every day for a month, and then go see somebody who always manages to upset you or make you defensive. See if they can *still* press your territorial retreat buttons.**

4. Spend a week-end at an Encounter Group. During the first half-day, try to intuit which quadrant each participant is coming from. At the end, see if any of them have become less robotized. See if *you* have become less robotized.

5. Go to the Lion House at the zoo. Study the lions until you feel you really understand *their* tunnel-reality.

6. Go to see the kind of comedy that small children like -- the Three Stooges, Abbott & Costello, etc. Observe carefully, and think about what function this humor serves; but don't neglect to laugh at it yourself.

7. Spend all day Sunday looking at animal shows on TV (getting stoned on weed, if this is permissible to you). Then go into the office the next day and observe the primate pack hierarchy *carefully,* like a scientist.

---

*Opiates and *small* does of alcohol seem to trigger neurotransmitters characteristic of Circuit 1 breast-fed tranquility. *Large* doses of alcohol often reverse this and trigger neurotransmitters characteristic of territorial struggle. Note the anal vocabulary of hostile drunks as their alcoholic intake increases.

**A good new book on Meditation is *Undoing Yourself With Energized Meditation And Other Devices,* by Christopher S. Hyatt. This book is published by FALCON PRESS.

CHAPTER FIVE

DICKENS AND JOYCE
THE ORAL-ANAL
DIALECTIC

That why all parks up excited about his
gunnfodder. That why ecrazyaztecs and crime
ministers preaching him mornings.

James Joyce
Finnegans Wake

THE GRACIOUS GODDESS AND THE TERRIFYING GIANT HAUNT OUR LEGENDS AND OUR LITERATURE.

**Hearasay in paradox lust.
Joyce, Finnegans Wake**

The shock and dismay of the infant when the harshness of traditional toilet training introduces the anal-Patrist second circuit values into the previously blissful oral-Matrist continuum is conveyed with great artistry in Dickens' *David Copperfield*. So overt is this sequence, indeed, that it is hard to believe it was actually written half a century before Freud's clinical writings.

Dickens describes an idyllic infanthood in which David lives with a widowed mother who can safely be characterized as a human embodiment of the *bona dea* (good goddess) of the ancients (who lingers still as the "fairy godmother" in children's tales). Onto this happy scene intrudes the horrible step-father Mr. Murdstone whose "Jehovah complex" makes him an avatar of the punishing father-god. There is no way of obeying all of Murdstone's rules; there are too many of them, and they are mostly unstated and implicit anyway. David undergoes some monumental *lashings on the buttocks* (for his own good, of course, although Dickens emphasizes in a quite Freudian way the obvious enjoyment Murdstone obtains from these sessions). Quite naturally, David begins to internalize this anal system of values and imagines he is quite a guilty little wretch and richly deserves this torture. Then Dickens inserts the following scene, when David returns from a year at school:

> I went in with quiet, timid step. God knows how infantile the memory may have been that was awakened in me at the sound of my mother's voice in the old parlour when I set foot in the hall. I think I must have laid in her arms and heard her singing to me when I was but a baby. The strain was new to me but it was so old that it filled my heart brimful like a friend come back from a long absence.
>
> I believed from the solitary and thoughtful way in which my mother murmered her song that she was alone, and I went softly into the room. She was sitting by the fire, suckling an infant whose tiny hand she held against her neck. Her eyes were looking down upon its face and she sat singing to it. I was so far right that she had no other companion. I spoke to her and she started and cried out. But seeing me she called me her dear Davy, her own boy: and coming half way across the room to meet me, kneeled down upon the ground and kissed me, and laid my head down on her bosom near the little creature that was nestling there, and put its hand up to my lips.
>
> I wish I had died. I wish I had died then, with that feeling in my heart. I should have been more fit for heaven than I have ever been since.

The dream of return to oral bio-security is too overt to require commentary.

Similarly, in Joyce's monumental novel of the mind of a man asleep, *Finnegans Wake*, the Father and the Father-God are always associated with war and excretion, as Joyce scholar William York Tindall has noted. As "Gunn, the Farther," the terrifying anal monster combines pistol, deity and flatulence; as "Delude of Israel," he is the jealous (territorial) Old Testament "Lord of Hosts," i.e. of battles. His insignia, the hundred letter thunder-word which recurs ten times in the dream, always combines Fatherhood, menace, defecation and war: for instance, in its first appearance on page 1, it is:

> bababalalgharaghtakamminaronnkonnbronnton
> nerronntounnthunntrovarrhounawnskawn
> toohoohoondenthurnuk

Here we find *Baba* (Arabic, father), phonetic *Abba* (Hebrew, father), phonetic *Canbronne* (the general who so appropriately said *merde* when asked to surrender the territory), phonetic Gaelic *scan* (crack: of thunder or of the anus), *ronnen* (Germanic, excretion), the suggestive *orden* implying both Germanic medal for valor and English *ordure*, etc. The terrifying Father-God elsewhere "Makes his manuvres in open ordure" and preaches all the anal-authoritarian values: "No cods before me... Thou shalt not commix idolatry . . . Love my label like myself." He is the villain of the *"goddinpotty"* (garden party) -- the trickster-god who set the baited trap in the Garden of Eden; the ego internalized in toilet-training (potty); the god of thunder and wrath (god-din).

Fleeing him, the "unhappitants of earth" always seek his opposite, ALP (German, dream; also the root of the first letters of the Greek and Hebrew alphabets -- *alpha* and *aleph,* the source, the beginning) -- Anna Livia Plurabella, when her name is written in full: the waters of life combined with all beautiful women. She is as oral and loving as "the Omniboss" is anal and threatening:

> with a beak, with a spring, all her rillringlets shaking, rock drops in her tachie, tramtokens in her hair, all waived to a point and then all inuendation, little oldfashioned mummy, little wonderful mommy, ducking under bridges . . .as happy as the day is wet, babbling, bubbling, chattering to herself, deloothering the fields . . .

This amniotic river-woman is the perfect mother of infantile dream memory and the Great Goddess of the ancients, the ideal bio-survival safe, warm place and to her Joyce offers his most fervent prayer:

> In the name of Annah the Allmaziful, the Everliving, the Bringer of Plurabilites, haloed be her eve, her singtime sung, her rill be run, unhemmed as it is uneven!

Humanity, in Joyce's view as in Rattray Taylor's, is forever leaving her to follow the Hero (Father) to "the bloodiedfilth of Waterloo" (battlefield of Waterloo with blood and excrement superimposed to reveal the anal-territorial roots of war) and then returning, temporarily chastened, "to list, as she bibs us, by the waters of babalong."

In Chapter Three of *Finnegans Wake,* the "offenders" (invaders) and "defenders" (natives) get so thoroughly mixed up that all that remains is a composite "fender" who takes the blame for everybody.

This cyclical view of history, whether in Joyce, Rattray Taylor, Vico (Joyce's source), Hegel-and-Marx, etc. is only part of the truth, but it needs to be stressed because it is the part that most people fearfully refuse to recognize. Whether we speak in terms of Taylor's Matrist-Patrist dialectic, Vico's cycle of Divine, Heroic and Urbanized ages, the Marx-Hegel trinity of Thesis-Antithesis-Synthesis, or any variation thereon, we are speaking of a pattern that is real and that does repeat.

But it only does so to the extent that people are robotized: trapped in hard-wired reflexes.

When the accumulated facts, gimmicks, tools, techniques and gadgets of neuro-science -- the science of brain change and brain liberation -- reaches a certain critical mass, we will all be able to free ourselves from these robot cycles. It is the thesis of this book that we have been approaching that critical mass for several decades now and will reach the cross-over point in less than ten years.

The current rampages of territorial-emotional pugnacity sweeping this planet are not just another civilization falling, Vico fashion.

PROMETHEUS RISING

They are the birth-pangs of a cosmic Prometheus rising out of the long nightmare of domesticated primate history.

The gracious goddess/hostile giant archetypes are not activated in cases where the mother is cold, rejecting, embittered etc. and the father is the warm, supportive figure. The imprints on the first and second circuits are statistically deviant in such families and anything may result -- a shaman, a schizophrenic, a genius, a homosexual, an artist, a psychologist, etc.

EXERCIZE

In terms of the theory so far developed, analyze the following characters:

1. Scarlett O'Hara
2. King Kong
3. Odysseus
4. Hamlet
5. Bugs Bunny
6. Portnoy
7. Leopold Bloom
8. Richard M. Nixon
9. Thomas Jefferson
10. St. Paul
11. Donald Duck
12. Iago
13. Jane Eyre
14. Josef Stalin
15. Joan of Arc
16. Timothy Leary
17. Aleister Crowley
18. The Author
19. Mao
20. Carl Jung
21. The Secret Chiefs

CHAPTER SIX

THE TIME-BINDING
SEMANTIC
CIRCUIT

It says that when you put two minds together, there is always a third mind, a third and superior mind, as an unseen collaborator.

William S. Burroughs and Brion Gysin,
The Third Mind

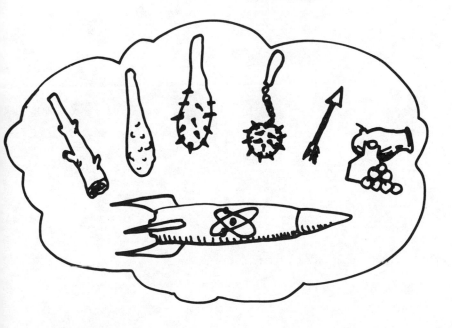

HUMAN BEINGS ARE TIME-BINDERS

The third, semantic circuit handles artifacts and makes a "map" (reality-tunnel) which can be passed on to others, even across generations. These "maps" may be paintings, as in illustrations, or words, concepts, tools (with instructions on use transmitted verbally), theories, music, etc.

Human beings (*domesticated*) primates are symbol-using crea-tures; which means, as the pioneer semanticist, Korzybski, noted, that *those who rule symbols rule us.*

If Moses, Confucius, Buddha, Mohammed, Jesus and St. Paul can be considered living influences -- and they are: look around the world -- this is only because their Signal has been carried to us by human symbol systems. These systems include words, artworks, music, rituals and unrecognized rituals ("games") through which culture is transmitted. Marx and Hitler, Newton and Socrates, Shakespeare and Jefferson, etc. continue to "rule" parts of humanity in the same way -- through the semantic circuit.

We are ruled even more, and even less consciously, by the inventors of the wheel, the plow, the alphabet, even the Roman roads.

Since words contain both *denotations* (referents in the sensory-existential world) and *connotations* (emotional tones and poetic or rhetorical hooks), humans can be moved to action even by words which have no real meaning or reference in actuality. This is the mechanism of demagoguery, advertising and much of organized religion.

The bio-survival circuit only divides experience into two sets: that which is good for me or nourishing, and that which is bad for me or threatening. The emotional-territorial circuit also divides the world into two halves: that which is more powerful than me (higher in the pecking order) and that which is less powerful than me (lower in the pecking order). On this basis sociobiological systems evolve and animal "societies" of truly human complexity have been studied.

The semantic circuit allows us to sub-divide things, and re-connect things, *at pleasure.* There is no end to its busy-busy-busy labelling and packaging of experience. On the personal level, this is the "internal monologue" discovered by Joyce in *Ulysses.* On the historical level, this is the *time-binding function* described by Korzybski, which allows each generation to add new categories to our mental library -- connecting new things, separating new things, reclassifying and reshuffling forever. In this time-binding dimension, Einstein replaced Newton before most of the world* had heard of Newton; simple arithmetic gave birth to algebra, which brought forth calculus, which produced tensor calculus,

*Most of the world was illiterate until the last decade.

etc. Haydn and Mozart prepared the way for Beethoven, who broke into the realms that the Romantics and Wagnerians took over, which gave birth to what is called music today.

So-called "future shock" has always been with us, since the semantic circuit began functioning somewhere in pre-history. In a symbolizing, calculating, abstracting species, all times are "times of change." The process is however *accelerating faster as time passes,* because the symbolizing faculty is inherently self-augmenting.

In ordinary language, the semantic circuit is usually called "the mind." (As psychologist Robert Ornstein said in a recent radio show, when we say someone "has a good mind," we generally mean they have *a good mouth,* i.e. they use the semantic circuit well.)

In terms of Transactional Analysis, the first (oral) circuit is called the Natural Child, the second (emotional) circuit is called the Adapted Child, and the semantic circuit is called the Adult or Computer. In Jungian terms, the first circuit mediates *sensation,* the second circuit *feeling,* and the third circuit *reason.*

The neurological components of the first circuit go back to the oldest parts of the brain; Carl Sagan calls these functions "the reptile brain." These neural structures are at least billions of years old. The second circuit structures appeared with the first amphibians and mammals, somewhere around 1000 million or 500 million years ago; Sagan calls them "the mammalian brain." The semantic circuit appeared perhaps 100 thousand years ago; Sagan calls it "the human brain." It should be no surprise that most people, most of the time, are controlled more by the older reptilian-mammalian circuits than by the human semantic (rational) circuit, or that the semantic circuit is so easily perverted into false logics (bigotries, intolerant ideologies, fanaticisms of all sorts) when the bio-survival circuit signals threat to life or the emotional circuit flashes threat to status.

Cynics, satirists and "mystics" (circuit V-VIII types) have told us over and over that "reason is a whore," i.e. that the semantic circuit is notoriously vulnerable to manipulation by the older, more primitive circuits. However much the Rationalist may resent this, it is always true in the short run -- that is, to use one of the Rationalist's favorite words, it is always *pragmatically* true.

Whoever can scare people enough (produce bio-survival anxiety) can sell them quickly on any verbal map that seems to give them relief, i.e. cure the anxiety. By frightening people with Hell and then offering them Salvation, the most ignorant or crooked individuals can "sell" a whole system of thought that cannot bear two minutes of rational analysis. And any domesticated primate alpha male, however cruel or crooked, can rally the primate tribe behind him by howling that a rival alpha male is about to lead his gang in an attack on this habitat. These two mammalian reflexes are known, respectively, as Religion and Patriotism. They work for domesticated primates, as for the wild primates, because they are Evolutionary Relative Successes. (So far.)

The emotional-territorial or "patriotic" circuit also contains the pack's status programs or pecking order. Working in tandem with first circuit bio-survival anxieties, it is always able to pervert the functioning of the semantic-rational circuit. Whatever threatens loss of status, and whatever invades one's "space" (including one's ideological "head space"), is a threat to the average domesticated primate. Thus, if a poor man has one status prop in his life -- "I'm a white man, not a goddam nigger" or "I'm normal, not a goddam faggot" or whatever -- any attempt to preach* tolerance, common humanity, relativism, etc. is not processed through the semantic circuit but through the emotional circuit, and is rejected as an attack on status (ego, social role).

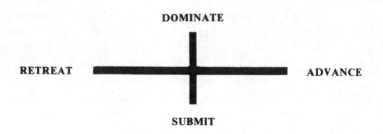

DOMINATE

RETREAT   ADVANCE

SUBMIT

*Of course, preaching itself is bad second circuit politics, since it puts you one-up on the person preached-at. You are *not* one-up unless imprinted as such by being an alpha male in the same gene-pool or conditioned as such by being a "boss" or other authority-figure. The counter-culture of the 1960s, like many other idealistic movements, failed because it did so much *preaching* from a morally one-up postion when nobody had been imprinted or conditioned to accept it as one-up.

The attentive reader will remember that the grid of the first two circuits puts the pre-verbal child in a two-dimensional world, which in the simplest of our diagrams looked like this (see proceeding page).

The third, semantic circuit seems intimately connected with three dimensionality (although our binocular vision, of course, also plays a role here). Specifically, right-handedness is a human, or at least a primate, trait. Other mammals show no right-hand preference; they are ambidextrous.

Recent neurology has shown that our *right-handedness* is intimately connected with our tendency to use the *left hemisphere of the brain* more than the right. (The left-handed minority are discussed below). Indeed, we use the right hemisphere so little in ordinary life that for a long time it was called "the silent hemisphere."

Thus, there is a genetic (hard-wired) preference, in most humans, for *right-handed manipulations* and *left-brain* mentations. Now these connections seem intimately involved with our verbal, semantic circuitry, because the left brain is the "talking" brain. It is linear, analytical, computer-like and very verbal. Thus, there is a neurological basis for the linkage between *mapping* and *manipulating*. The right hand *manipulates* the universe (and makes artifacts) and the left-brain *maps* the results into a model, which allows for predictions about future behavior of that part of the universe. These are the distinctly *human* (post-primate) characteristics.

The left-handed, on the contrary, specialize in right-brain functions, which are holistic, supra-verbal, "intuitive," musical and "mystical." Leonardo, Beethoven and Nietzsche, for instance, were all left-handed. Traditionally, left-handed people have been the subject of both dread and awe -- regarded as weird, shamanic, and probably in special communication with "God" or "the Devil."*

There is thus a cross-over which makes for a left-right polarity in both brain-functioning and hand-functioning, each being a reverse mirror image of the other:

---

*Aleister Crowley knew about this *pragmatically*, before modern neurology. He taught his pupils to learn to write equally well with both hands, thereby forcing the dormant right brain to spring to activity.

LEFT BRAIN
(analysis)
(Circuit III)

RIGHT BRAIN
(intuition)
(Circuit VI)

Left Hand   Right Hand

This double (and reversed) right-left polarity places us neurologically in three-dimensional space. Re-arranging our diagram and adding the third circuit, we can illustrate the mind-field as follows:

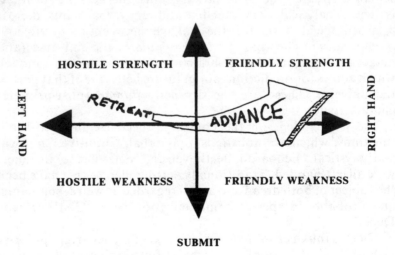

DOMINATE

HOSTILE STRENGTH   FRIENDLY STRENGTH

LEFT HAND   RETREAT   ADVANCE   RIGHT HAND

HOSTILE WEAKNESS   FRIENDLY WEAKNESS

SUBMIT

To visualize this two-dimensional sketch of a three-dimensional system it is necessary to imagine that the advance-retreat axis is at right angles to the others -- that is, "see" it coming out of the page at you.

This is "Euclidean" space. It is obvious, in this context, why

Euclidean space was the first kind of space discovered by mathematicians, and by artists, and why it still seems "natural" to us; why some have great difficulty in imagining the non-Euclidean kinds of space used in modern physics.

Euclidean space is a *projection outward* of the way our nervous systems stacks information on the bio-survival, emotional and semantic circuits.

Thus, the imprint sites of this circuit are located in the *left cortex* and closely linked with the delicate muscles of *larynx* and the fine manipulations of *right-handed* "dexterity." The cortex itself is so recent in evolution that it is often called "the new brain;" it is found only in the higher mammals and is most developed in humans and cetaceans (dolphins and whales).

Those extreme cases who take their heaviest imprint on the third circuit tend to grow up cerebrotonic. They are tall and skinny, because energy is perpetually drawn upward from the body into the head. The caricatured evil genius, Dr. Sylanus in Superman, who was virtually all head, represents the extreme toward which this type seems to be evolving. Popular speech calls them "eggheads."

Almost always, these cerebrotonic Third Circuit types ignore or are hostile to their first and second circuit functions. Playfulness puzzles them (appears silly or eccentric) and emotions both baffle and frighten them.

Since we all contain this circuit, we all need to exercize it regularly. Make up a schematic diagram of your business or home and try to streamline it for more efficiency. Design a chart that explains the whole universe. Every few years, study a science you know nothing about, at an Adult Education center.

And don't neglect to *play* with this circuit: write poems, jingles, fables, proverbs or jokes.

**REMEMBER MR. CROWLEY SAID
YOU TOO ARE A STAR
P.S. HE ALSO SAID ——— DO NOT
LUST
AFTER RESULTS**

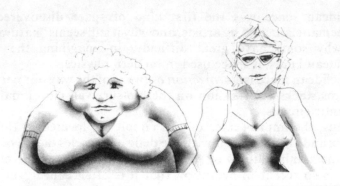

VISCEROTONIC
EXTREME
Circuit I
Imprint
Jung's feeling type
"Natural Child"

MUSCULOTONIC
EXTREME
Circuit II
Imprint
Jung's sensational type
"Adapted Child"

CEREBROTONIC
EXTREME
Circuit III
Imprint
Jung's rational type
"Adult or Computer"

THE NEUROLOGICAL IMPRINT IS THE BLUE-PRINT FOR THE ENTIRE ORGANISM

As with the earlier circuits, the semantic circuit builds all of its conditioning and learning onto a bedrock of hard-wired imprinting. Thus, many existentially thinkable thoughts are socially *un*thinkable, since (a) everybody in a given society has roughly the same semantic imprint and (b) this is reinforced daily by assumptions that are mechanically taken for granted.

Thus, a genius is one who, by some internal process, breaks through to Circuit VII -- a minor neurological miracle loosely called "intuition" -- and comes back down to the third circuit with the capacity to paint a new semantic map, build a new model of experience. Needless to say, this is always a profound shock to those still trapped in the old robot-imprints, and is generally considered a threat to territory (ideological head space). The long list of martyrs to free enquiry, from Socrates onward, shows how mechanical this *neophobia* (fear of new semantic signals) is.

As Thomas Kuhn showed in *The Structure of Scientific Revolutions,* science itself -- the apotheosis of third circuit semantic rationality -- is not free of this neophobia. Kuhn demonstrated, at length, that each scientific revolution took one full generation to turn over the old world view. And Kuhn further showed that the older scientists *never* are converted to the new semantic paradigm. They are, in our terminology, mechanically hooked to their original imprints. The revolution is complete, as Kuhn shows, only when a second generation, not hooked to the old imprint, is able to compare the two models and decides rationally that the newer one really does make more sense.

But if science, the most self-correcting of all information-processing third circuit functions, has this one-generation time lag, what can be said of politics, religion, economics? Time-lags of centuries, or even milleniums, are common there.*

We commented earlier that in bio-survival neurology, there is *no time.* "I just found myself doing it," we say after passing through an automatic reflex on the bio-survvival circuit.

Emotional-territorial circuit actions begin to include time as a factor. Dominance signals may not "work": the seemingly weaker mammal may offer a counter-challenge. Two dogs will walk around each other for several minutes growling and sniffing

---

*This only refers to *other people's* politics, religions and economics, needless to say. The reader's own opinions on these subjects are the only reasonable and objective ones. Of course.

79

(the chemical secretions of each reveals its actual degree of fear to the other) before Top Dog and Bottom Dog becomes clear.

On the human level, we often agonize over emotional decisions, becoming acutely conscious of *time* as we hesitate. As every suspense writer knows, the principle way to increase emotional tension is to set a *time limit* on a difficult or dangerous decision. (See any *Star Trek* script; the time-limit is never missing. Or see any of Irving Wallace's bestsellers. Suspense is always increased, of course, if the time-limit is abruptly shortened just before the climax.)

On the third circuit, time becomes *conceptualized* as well as *experienced*. We know ourselves as creatures of time; the "tale of the tribe," the totem pole, the *Odyssey* of Homer, the *Old Testament*, the *Vedas*, etc. tell us what came before and often contains prophecies of what will come later. Science expands the third circuit into contemplation of time-spans that stagger our imaginations. The very use of written languages and other symbols like mathematics creates the time-binding sense of Korzybski: we know ourselves as receivers of messages sent by sages "of olde" and as potential transmitters of messages that may be scanned ages in the future.

The fourth circuit causes us to be even more involved in, and *pressured* by, time.

In closing this chapter let us be reminded that Giordano Bruno was burned at the stake February 18, 1600, for teaching that the earth moves. Was he **guilty** or **not**?

EXERCIZES

1. If you are a Liberal, subscribe to the *National Review,* the country's most intelligent (and witty) conservative magazine, for a year. Each month try to enter their reality-tunnel for a few hours while reading their articles.

2. If you are a Conservative, subscribe to the *New York Review of Books* for a year and try to get into their head-space for a few hours a month.

3. If you are a Rationalist, subscribe to *Fate* magazine for a year.

4. If you are an occultist, join the Society for the Scientific

Investigation of Claims of the Paranormal and read their journal, *The Skeptic*, for a year.

5. Buy a copy of the *Scientific American* and read any article in it. Ask the following questions: Why do they sound so sure? Does the data support dogmatism at this point, or is dogma *a primate habit* (defending head-space)? Will these theories still be believed in 1999? In 2011? In 2593?

6. Get into a discussion of philosophy with an educated Marxist, an intelligent Moslem and a Japanese businessman at the first opportunity.

7. Buy some ZOOM or LIFT (two names for the same caffeine-high stimulant) at a Health Food Store. (This gives a close approximation of the effects of illegal cocaine.) When you are Zooming or Lifted and your mind is racing, find a victim and explain the universe to him or her, until they are able to escape you.

What you experience in this "speed rap" is what the head of the compulsive Rationalist is *always* like. This is the verbal circuit gone wild and totally oblivious to information coming in on any other circuit. It explains why most people cannot stand Rationalists. "Speed" drugs evidently trigger neurotransmitters characteristic of the verbal centers of the left cortex.

CHAPTER SEVEN

THE TIME-BINDING DIALECTIC: ACCELERATION AND DECELERATION

In the dialectic between nature and the socially constructed world, the human organism is transformed. In this dialectic man produces reality and thereby produces himself.

Berger and Luckman,
The Social Construction of Reality

The first and second circuits are Evolutionary Stable Strategies. They have worked, in more or less the same form, not just for primates but for other mammals, and for many other species, over vast aeons of time.

The third, semantic circuit is an Evolutionary Unstable Strategy. It could very accurately be called *revolutionary* rather than *evolutionary*.

The first two circuits are based on *positive feedback,* in the biological sense. They maintain *homeostasis* -- that is, they return, over and over, to the same ecological-ethological balances. The function of positive feedback is to return to such a steady state.

The time-binding semantic circuit is not based on such steady-state positive feedback. It is a mechanism of what cyberneticists and biologists called *negative feedback.* It does not return to a steady state, but constantly seeks a new equilibrium at a higher energy level. (Positive feedback returns to a fixed point, like a thermostat. Negative feedback seeks a moving goal, like a guided missile.)

The first two circuits maintain that which is (more or less) constant in human affairs. They are totally *cyclical*, and relate directly to the cycles found in history by Vico, Hegel and similar philosophers.

The third circuit has always been hemmed-in and heavily sanctioned with rules, laws, prohibitions, taboos, etc. because it breaks up such cycles. It leads, if unleashed, to an upward-hurtling spiral.

In oooiotion where the third, semantic circuit has been partially unleashed -- it has never been totally freed in any society -- the upward spiral immediately appears. This used to be known as "progress," before that word became unfashionable.

The upward spiral (whether we call it "progress" or not) is characteristic of what Karl Popper calls Open Societies. These are secular, humanistic societies -- cultures *relatively* free of taboo and dogmatism.

Such freedom, up to and including the present, is only *relative*, because many taboos are unconscious and pass themselves off as "common sense" or "common decency," etc. Whoever challenges them is by definition a "heretic," by definition a "traitor," or by definition "an irresponsible nut."

(Rationalists, who dominate in *relatively* Open Societies, also have their own taboos, as we shall see.)

It was historian Henry Adams who first conceived the idea that there might be a mathematical expression describing the rate of change of human societies.

Under the influence of Newton's physics, Adams suggested --and he was very tentative about this: a fact to be remembered by those who ridicule his "naivete" -- that the utilization of energy might move forward as the inverse square of *time,* just as Newton's gravity functions as the inverse square of *distance.*

Accepting the anthropology of his day, Adams assumed humanity in its present form was about 90,000 plus years old. He then reckoned that it took most of that time to arrive at Galileo, the scientific method, the beginnings of the Industrial Revolution, and the great leap forward in energy utilization characteristic of the "modern" age, or the Open Society.

Since 300 is the inverse square of 90,000, Adams assumed that the next great leap was happening while he was writing, around 1900 -- 300 years after Galileo. Looking about him, he decided this next jump to higher energy was occurring in the researches of the Curies, who had discovered radioactivity. As many commentators have noted, it is impossible to read Adams on this subject without feeling that he is very accurately forecasting the Atomic Age.

Adams went further, with the exhilaration of a great idea. Since 17 plus is the inverse square of 300, he predicted that the next great evolutionary stage would begin in 1917 plus. And, since the inverse square of 17 is 4 plus, he predicted the next step in around 1922. By then, he said, we should have infinite energy at our disposal. It didn't quite work out that way.

Nevertheless, Henry Adams was on the right track. His math was just over-simplified.

Also "on the right track" was Henry's brother, Brooks, who was also looking for "laws" in history. Brooks observed a pattern which may or may not be *entirely* true but is as approximately true as the similar generalizations of Vico, Hegel, Marx and Toynbee. Every civilization, Brooks Adams proposed, goes through four stages:

1. The *monopolization of knowledge* by priests. e.g., the Egyptian priests kept written language a secret among themselves,

as did the Mayan priests.

2. The *monopolization of military power* by conquerors who made themselves States or governments. e.g., "a French bastard" (Tom Paine's description of William the Conqueror) lands on the shore of England with a superior technology -- warriors on horse versus native warriors on foot -- and he becomes King. His relatives and sycophants become Lords-of-the-land.

3. The *monopolization of the land* by these land-Lords. The extraction of tribute ("rent") from those who live on the land.

4. The *monopolization of the issue of currency* by National Banks. The extraction of tribute ("interest") for each piece of currency put into circulation.

Most civilizations seem to have gone through at least three of these stages, not always consecutively. Some have passed through all four.

Brooks Adams also noted that *centralized capital* (the accumulation of wealth in the hands of a few inter-related families) seems to have been moving steadily West throughout recorded history. The first major accumulations are to be found in Sumer; the center of money-power then shifted to Egypt, to Greece, to the Italian peninsula, to various parts of Germany, and then to London. At the time Brooks Adams was writing (c. 1900) he saw the balance teetering between London and New York, and he predicted that the decline of the English Empire would shift the balance to New York within the first half of the 20th Century. He seems to have been right. Brooks Adams had *no theory* as to why this Westward movement of wealth had been going on for 6000 years. He merely observed the pattern.

The shift is still continuing, in the opinion of many. For instance, Carl Oglesby in *The Cowboy vs. Yankee War*, sees American politics since 1950 dominated by a struggle between "old Yankee wealth" (the New York-Boston axis, which replaced London after 1900) and "new Cowboy wealth" (Texas-California oil-and-aerospace billionaires). As of 1980, it looks like the Cowboys are winning; which is what one would expect if there were a real "law" behind Adams' East-West migration of capital.

One night in 1919, Count Alfred Korzybski awoke from a vivid dream, tears of joy streaming down his face, with a vivid sense that the passing of signals from generation to generation -- the third circuit time-binding function -- was what distinguished us from the other primates.

Korzybski originally suggested that time-binding could be defined mathematically. He dropped this idea later -- his math was as inadequate as Henry Adam's -- but it is worth looking at for a moment, to retrace the steps by which the actual Law of Acceleration was discovered.

What Korzybski assumed at first was that if all the inventions, discoveries, etc. of some hypothetical first generation of humans could be represented by P, and the rate by which the second generation could surpass this by R, then, mathematically, the sum total of inventions, discoveries etc. at the end of the second generation would be PR. Quite true, algebraically. Then, after a third generation, the stockpile would be PRR. And after four generations, PRRR.

Generalized, this becomes PR^t, where (t) is the number of generations from whatever generation you have picked as your base-line.

The curve of PR^t, if you put it on graph paper, ascends more rapidly with each generation. Korzybski was looking straight at what Alvin Toffler later called "Future Shock" and was trying to write a mathematical formula for it.

Many variables in economic-technological history do, in fact, fit Korzybski's PR^t funtion; but others do not. The math, again, was too simple; and *everything does not change at the same rate.* Nonetheless, Korzybski, like Henry Adams, was groping toward the truth: acceleration is real, and it is intimately connected with *time-binding,* the passing of signals between generations.

What underlies the accelerations noted by Henry Adams and Korzybski is nowadays known as the selection of *negentropy* out of *stochastic processes.* Our understanding of this is chiefly due to almost-simultaneous discoveries (1946-48) by quantum physicist Erwin Schrödinger, mathematician Norbert Weiner and an electronics-communication expert at Bell Laboratories, Claude Shannon.

A stochastic process is a random series, but it is a special kind of random series. In a stochastic process, some agent or agency is making selections -- picking out of the randomness a pattern that is not random.

A *pattern that is not random* is known mathematically as information.

Information can also be defined as organization, or as coherence.

Gregory Bateson has defined information as "differences that make a difference."

Information -- coherence -- "differences that make a difference" Korzybski's *Time-Binding* -- these are all aspects of the *unpredictable*. If you know something already, or can predict it easily on the basis of what you do know, it is not information for you. Conversely, if you don't know something, or can't predict it, it *is* information.

The dynamism of evolution, we repeat, is the selection of information, coherence, out of a random series of events. The emergence of information can be illustrated crudely by the following three poemlets:

Roses are red
Violets are blue
Sugar is sweet
And so are you

Unless the reader has lived in relative isolation from American-English folk-culture, this poem had very little information for him. You could guess what was coming every step of the way. But consider by contrast:

Roses are red
Ink is black
Do me a favor
Go sit on a tack

This crude jest (of grade school origin) has more information for more readers, because it is less predictable. Another leap in information-content occurs in Steve Allen's:

Roses are red
Violets are blue
You think this will rhyme
But it ain't gonna

The humorous unpredictability of this poem gives it, mathematically, a higher information level than the predictable Valentine poem we started with. If this is still obscure, try it in terms of Bateson's elegant simplification "information is difference that makes a difference."

Information is also known mathematically as negative entropy or, in a widely used abbreviation, negentropy. Entropy is a measure of the deadness of a system. Negentropy or information is a measure of the liveliness of a system. Evolution is always a matter of *at least* two stochastic processes, each one acting as "selector" of the other (s). That is, in non-living systems, where no such "selection" is involved, entropy (lack of coherence) steadily increases, as stated in the famous Second Law of Thermodynamics. In living systems, due to stochastic co-selection, negentropy (information) steadily increases. In Schrödinger's phrase, "Life *feeds* on negative entrophy." *Life is an ordering, selecting, coherence-making process.*

Without getting embroiled in metaphysics, life (evolution) behaves *as if* it were always aiming at higher coherence, i.e. higher intelligence.

This process accelerates because it is, as Shannon demonstrated mathematically, logarithmic. Logarithmic processes are such that if you put them on graph paper, the curve rises more and more all the time.

Hence, the accelerations noted by Adams and Korzybski are human increments in a process that has been innate in evolution all along.

The human increment accelerates faster than pre-human evolution because *through the third, semantic circuit* and its symbols (words, maps, equations etc.) we are able to pass information (negative entropy: coherence) from generation to generation.

World-wide wealth in terms of "Real Capital" (plants in actual known resources etc.) has been *doubling every generation* since economists started collecting statistics in the 18th Century.

Where does this wealth come from? According to orthodox economists it comes from land, labor, and capital. According to Marxists, it comes from land and labor alone, and the capitalist is a thief who has inserted an artificial bookkeeping system into the process. *Both are wrong.* Land and labor alone, and land - labor and capital together, can't produce new wealth if they are all organized by a fallacious idea, such as searching for oil where oil is not. The real source of wealth is correct ideas: workable ideas:

that is, negative entropy -- Information.

The origin of these coherent (workable) ideas is the human nervous system. *All wealth is created by human beings using their neurons intelligently.*

A neurotic young man once went to a Zen Master and asked how he could find peace of mind.

"How can you lack anything," the *Roshi* asked "when you own the greatest treasure in the universe?"

"How do I own the greatest treasure in the universe?" asked the young man, baffled.

"The place that question comes from is the greatest treasure in the universe," said the Master, being more explicit than is common for a Zen teacher.

Of course, as a Buddhist, the Master had taken a vow of poverty and did not mean exactly what we mean here. But he knew that the brain produces all that we experience -- all our pain and worry, all our bliss states and ecstasies, all our higher evolutionary vistas and trans-time Peak Experiences, etc. It is also "the greatest treasure in the universe" in the most materialistic economic sense: it creates all the *ideas* which, socially employed, become wealth: roads, scientific laws, calendars, factories, computers, life-saving drugs, medicines, ox-carts, autos, jet planes, spaceships . . .

If you are not alone in the wilderness, lift your eyes from the page and look about. All that you see, whoever theoretically "owns" it, is the time-binding product of the materialized or manifested ideas of creative men and women. It is all negative entropy. Coherent order.

And it is moving toward higher and more coherent order at a faster rate-of-change all the time.

Of course, if you *are* alone in the wilderness, you will also see coherent order, but in this case, the rate-of-change toward higher order is much slower. That is, those stochastic processes which we call genetic drift, evolution etc. are co-selecting higher order at a different time rate than those stochastic processes which we call human thought, invention, culture etc. (This is why it is so hard to reach agreement about whether the natural processes are intelligent or not. As Bateson points out, if we accept any ordering process as intelligent, then the biosphere is indeed intelligent; but if we save the word "intelligence" only for those ordering processes that move at the same speed as our brains, then Nature is merely mechanical, not intelligent. To an extra-terrestrial with a different time-sense than ours, *this question would not arise at all.*)

Most of what we perceive in the human environment is made up of concretized ideas, in the above sense. Look again at a human community; you are seeing the historical human mind manifesting itself.

All ideas are not equally good, of course.

All manifested ideas (human creations in the biosphere) are, therefore, not equally good.

This is why John Ruskin, a century ago, tried to introduce a distinction between *wealth* and *illth*. This distinction did not become accepted and incorporated into our language because people, at that time, were not ready for it.

Wealth, in Ruskin's sense, consists of all those artifacts (concretized ideas) which enhance human life, or life generally. Illth consists of those artifacts which destroy, demean or degrade life. A factory that pollutes the air or water is illth in this sense; so is a bomb, a sword, a pistol, a tank of nerve-gas.

The Westward migration of Capital noted by Brooks Adams was a migration of both wealth and illth.

Obviously, under primitive planetary conditions -- finite space and finite resources -- the illth was perceived as necessary to protect the wealth. Territorial politics are much the same among domesticated primates as among other mammals; the primates are just smarter at building more omni-lethal weapons faster. This was originally a survival trait, an Evolutionary Relative Success, because primates are born without the physiological, inbuilt weaponry (lethal teeth, claws, horns etc.) of other mammals.

Since the Age of Reason in the 18th Century, the exponential increase in wealth (life-enhancing ideas manifesting) has led to more and more Utopian yearnings. At the same time, the equal and opposite increase in illth has led to more and more dystopian and apocalyptical fears.

One's expectations about the future -- utopia or dystopia -- are always based on what one thinks is the dominant force in evolution. This whole book, not just the present chapter, is based on the belief that an over-view of evolution shows beyond all doubt that wealth-producing faculty (the search for higher

CAPITAL HAS MOVED STEADILY WESTWARD BECAUSE NEW IDEAS ALWAYS APPEAR ON THE EXPANDING WAVE.

coherence) is the deciding factor. The illth-producing faculty is an archaic mammalian survival system rapidly becoming obsolete.

The highest historical concentration of wealth (real capital, and ideas generating new capital) now co-exists with the highest concentration of evolutionarily advanced nervous systems.

In California, Oregon, Alaska, British Columbia, Arizona, Texas, the Hawaiian Islands, Japan and all around the Pacific, where East meets West, the world of 1990 and 2000 and 2010 is being created by persons who are veterans of a gigantic Neurological Revolution -- the psychedelic pioneers of the 1960s, the graduates of the Consciousness Movement of the 1950s-70s, the synthesizers of modern psychology and ancient Oriental mind-sciences. These persons are called the Aquarian Conspiracy by Marilyn Ferguson, one of their spokespersons. They are denounced as the Me Generation by Tom Wolfe, a time-traveler from New York, i.e. from *the neurological past*, from a culture crystalized before 1950.

This "Me Generation" is the *temporary* high water mark of the time-binding function. Moving steadily Westward -- away from Tradition, away from Dogma -- they are the products, as Edmund Burke said of the first Americans, of "the dissidence of dissent and the Protestantism of the Protestants." Every heresy that left Europe produced newer, wilder heresies in the Eastern Seaboard, 1600-1800. Those that were "too far out" had to move further West and produced the 1000 Utopian communities (anarchist, evangelical, free-love etc.) that were attempted in the mid-West during the 19th Century. Those who were even further "out" -- out of the traditional mode -- moved further Westward in the last 30-70 years.

All of the fallout of this migration seems weird to the Eastern states, and even weirder to Europeans.

It all became much weirder still when it hit the Pacific and began to interact with Oriental neuro-sciences and brain-change arts, like yoga and Taoism and Zen.

It swallowed the Oriental lessons whole, without *becoming* Oriental *entirely*. It remained Western -- the dissidence of dissent etc. -- and it has been gaining momentum and direction for two or three decades now.

It aims at Higher Coherence and Higher Intelligence.

This is the new Power Elite.

As youngsters, these Aquarian Conspirators made the Youth Revolution of the 1960s, which -- whatever its excesses and blunders -- permanently changed and improved student-administrator-teacher feedback in our universities; liberated our Puritan culture for some healthy hedonism; imported a dozen varieties of Oriental neuro-science (and two dozen varieties of Oriental humbug, alas); launched the ecology movement (the first planetwide perception of the difference between *wealth* and *illth*); recreated a true love of the wilderness and of wild creatures; pioneered flex-time and other liberations from economic robothood;* launched Womens Lib, Gay Lib, Child Lib and generously supported Black Lib; ended the Vietnam War; spread holistic medicine throughout our culture; etc.

The same group is now leading the computer revolution; spearheading the drive toward Space Migration; supporting the Hunger Project, which will abolish starvation in our lifetimes; leading the Longevity revolution and the search for immortality; etc.

And they are all very conscious of being part of the Intelligence Intensification explosion which is the major topic of this book.

This type of "Western progressivism (or Utopianism) came out of the mid-East and is the distinct contribution of the Jews, which is why all reactionaries are intuitively anti-Semitic. As William Blake wrote of this tradition:

> **The Prophets Isaiah and Ezekiel dined with me, and I asked them how they dared so roundly to assert that God spoke to them; and whether they did not think at the time that they would be misunderstood & so be the cause of imposition.**
>
> **Isaiah answer'd: 'I saw no God, nor heard any, in a finite organical perception; but my senses discover'd the infinite in everything, and as I was then persuaded & remain confirmed that the voice of honest indignation is the voice of God, I cared not for consequences, but wrote.'**

This vision of the infinite in everything is common to East and West; what is distinctly Western, out of the Jews, is the voice of honest indignation against every institution which would deny or

---

*Virtually all the computer manufacturing firms in Silicon Valley (the peninsula south of San Francisco) have flex-time. The employees choose their own working hours.

demean the infinity within each human soul. The release of our full human potential -- to let the light of Prometheus shine everywhere -- is the distinctly *Western* mystic tradition and does not appear in Hinduism, Buddhism, Taoism or any Eastern religion.

Thomas Jefferson developed his view that "all men are created equal" from the perception of the infinity within each of us, which he learned from the Scottish philosophers, Reid and Hutcheson. (It was also from Hutcheson that Jefferson got his idea of "unalienable rights," which Congress in the interest of stylistic elegance altered to "inalienable rights.") The Scottish Enlightenment, like the French and English Enlightenment, was the beginning of the materialization and manifestation of the Judeo-Christian vision of the Heavenly City.

It was also this 18th Century Illuminati circle which introduced the concept of *progress* -- the conscious formulation of the symbolism of Prometheus. This vision has been under so much attack in recent decades that to defend it at all will seem archaic and eccentric to many readers.

Nonetheless, *evolution is real;* quantum jumps do occur throughout the biosphere and throughout human intellectual history. We are riding a mounting tidal wave of rising consciousness and expanding intelligence which is accelerating whether we like it or not.

By and large, most people -- and especially most ruling elites have not liked this acceleration factor. The migration of capital (i.e. *ideas*) Westward has been largely a flight from oppression, an escapist movement -- as critics today describe Space as "escapist." Everywhere, everywhen, the rulers of society have tried to put a brake on the third circuit, to *decelerate* the acceleration function, to establish limits on what was printable, discussable, even thinkable.

The Greek myth of Prometheus Bound -- the Titan who brought Light to humanity and is eternally punished for it -- is the synecdoche, the perfect symbol, of how the third circuit has been handled in most human societies.

The peculiar way most societies have imprinted the fourth, socio-sexual circuit -- the weird taboos which restrain us all, in every tribe, however technologically "advanced" -- is part of the acceleration-deceleration dialectic.

The fourth circuit has been largely imprinted to serve as a brake, holding back the free activity of the time-binding semantic circuit.

This is the historical function of taboos and "morality."

EXERCIZES

1. Compare Greece in the 4th Century B.C., Rome in the First Century A.D., Southern Europe at the beginning of the Renaissance, England c. 1600-1900, New York c. 1900-1950, and California today. Note the accumulation of wealth corresponding to the accumulation of heresies, innovations, cults, kooks, pioneers, inventors etc.

2. Imagine you put a penny on the first square of a chess-board, two cents on the second square, four cents on the third, etc. How much will you have to put on the sixty-fourth square? This is how time-binding works, in relatively Open Societies.

3. Read the denunciations of Galileo by the orthodox of his time.

4. Read the denunciations of Beethoven, of Picasso, of Joyce by those who knew in advance what music, painting and novels *should be.*

5. Are the most important scientific ideas of 1983 going to be published in *Scientific American* in 1983, or in 1993?

6. Research how many years passed between the publication of Einstein's paper on Special Relativity and the acceptance of the idea by the majority of physicists.

CHAPTER EIGHT

THE "MORAL" SOCIO-SEXUAL CIRCUIT

As the caterpillar chooses the fairest leaves to lay her eggs on, so the priest lays his curse on the fairest joys.

William Blake
Marriage of Heaven & Hell

The socio-sexual circuit is activated and imprinted at adolescence, when the DNA signal awakens the sexual apparatus. The teenager becomes the bewildered possessor of a new body and a new neural circuit oriented to orgasm and sperm-egg fusion. The pubescent human, like any other rutting animal, lurches about in a state of mating frenzy, every call gasping for the sexual object.

Imprint vulnerability is acute, and the first sexual signals to turn on the adolescent nervous system remain fixed for life and forever define the individual's sexual reality.

We should not be surprised, therefore, at the various fetishes that are so easily acquired at these sensitive moments.

In fact, we can tell precisely at what period in time a person was sexually imprinted by noting which fetishes continue to turn him or her on. *Black garters, booze, cool jazz,* and *crewcuts* define the sexual signals of one imprint group (generation) just as rigidly as *sleeping bags, marijuana, heavy rock* and *tight jeans* define another.

As Masters and Johnson have pointed out, most sexual dysfunctions are hooked into the nervous system at these adolescent moments of acute imprint vulnerability; their archetypal case is that of a male who, about to mate for the first time, in the backseat of a car, was traumatized by a policeman flashing a light on him and his paramour. The imprint of that ghastly moment was hooked for decades: the male remained impotent until reimprinted by Masters and Johnson in their clinic.

The choices of heterosexuality or homosexuality, brash promiscuity or timid celibacy, etc. are usually imprinted by exactly similar accidents at points of imprint vulnerability. Just as biosurvival anxiety or security are imprinted by accidents in the nursing period, emotional domination or submission by accidents in the toddling period, symbolic dexterity or "stupidity" by the accidents of the learning environment.

Primitives (so-called) know these facts and surround all the points of imprint vulnerability with rituals, "ordeals," "rites of passage," etc. well designed to imprint the desired traits of a well-integrated member of that tribe at that time. Relics of these imprint ceremonies survive in Baptism, Confirmation, Bar Mitzvahs, Marriage Ceremonies, the Masonic "raising," etc.

It is important to realize that chance, genetics and malice (anger) are among the "accidents" that create imprints at the points of vulnerability.

Most humans do not, due to accidents of this sort, imprint exactly the socio-sexual role demanded by their society. The fourth circuit can almost be called the *guilt circuit:* almost everybody, almost everywhere, is quite busy hiding their real sexual profile and miming the "accepted" sex role for their gender in their tribe.

In ordinary language, the imprint on the socio-sexual circuit is generally called "the mature personality" or the "sexual role." It is "the Parent" in the jargon of Transactional Analysis.

It is amusing to note that Freud recognized the first circuit as the oral stage, the second as the anal stage and the fourth as the genital stage. He did not notice the third, semantic circuit -- perhaps because as an obessive Rationalist he was so absorbed in verbal and conceptual programs that they were invisible to him, as water may be to fishes. Similarly, Jung described the first circuit as the *sensational* faculty, the second as the *feeling* faculty, the third as the *rational* faculty -- and skipped the socio-sexual circuit entirely. (There may be a clue here as to why Jung could not abide Freud's fourth circuit emphasis and built a separate, less sexual psychology of his own.) Jung then went on to lump all the higher circuits under the rubric of the faculty of *intuition*.

It is the function of the nervous system to focus, to select, to narrow down; to choose, from an infinity of possiblities, the biochemical imprints which determine the tactics and strategies that ensure survival in *one* place, status in *one* tribe.

The infant is genetically prepared to learn *any* language, master *any* skill, play *any* sex role; in a very short time, however, he or she becomes mechanically, robotically, fixated to accept, follow and mimic the limited offerings of his social and cultural environment.

In this process, each of us pays a **heavy price.** Survival and status mean forfeiting the infinite possibilities of unconditioned consciousness. The domesticated primate, inside the social reality-tunnel, is a trivial fragment of the potentials for experience and intelligence innate in the 110,000,000,000-cell human biocomputer. As Robert A. Heinlein writes:

A human being should be able to change a diaper, plan an invasion, butcher a hog, design a building, conn a ship, write a sonnet, balance accounts, build a wall, set a bone, comfort the dying, take orders, give orders, cooperate, act alone, solve an equation, analyze a new problem, pitch manure, program a computer, cook a tasty meal, fight efficiently, die gallantly. Specialization is for insects.

But as long as we remain on the antique circuits we are not very different from the insects. That is, just as the insects repeat their four-stage program (egg, larvae, chrysalis, adult) from generation to generation, we repeat our four-stage cycle also. The antique circuits are genetically conservative. They ensure the survival and continuation of the species, but do no more. For future evolution we must look to the futuristic circuits.

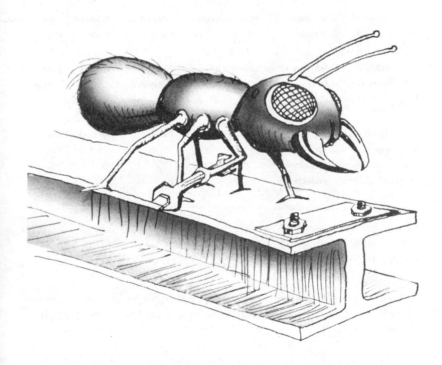

SPECIALIZATION IS FOR INSECTS

SUMMARY

CIRCUIT	ORIGIN	IMPRINT SITES	NAMES IN OTHER PSYCHOLOGIES					
I	3-4 billion years ago	Limbic & ANS	Freud Oral	Jung Sensation	Berne Natural Child	Sagan Reptile Brain	Gurdjieff* Movement Center
II	500-1000 mill. yrs.	Thalamus Muscles	Anal	Feeling	Adapted Child	Mammal Brain	False emotion Center
III	100,000 years ago	left cortex larynx right hand	Latency	Reason	Adult Computer	Human Brain	False intellect Center
IV	30,000 years ago	left neo-cortex breasts genitalia	Phallic	Ignored	Parent	Ignored	False Personality

*The Gurdjieff titles are deliberately negative, since he was trying to get people off these primitive circuits and into the futuristic circuits.

It is sometime mistakenly stated that there are no universal sexual taboos. This is not true. There is one omni-purpose taboo which exists in every tribe.

That taboo stipulates that sexuality shall *not* be unregulated by the tribe. That is, even though no other taboos are universal, the taboo against living without taboos remains constant. Every tribe has its own set of *verbots* and thou-shalt-nots, but no tribe allows the individual to choose his or her own set.

An American President may not marry his own sister (if he wants to get re-elected); an Egyptian Pharoh *had to* marry his own sister. Confronted by this moral relativism, many social scientists have failed to notice the invariable: both the President and the Pharaoh are expected to obey *local* rules. So are the Samoan, the Russian, the Eskimo and the Cuban.

Why is there this taboo against sexual self-definition and self-actualization? Why is it that, while no two societies can agree on what is sexually "good" and sexually "bad," every society thinks that it must make some definition?

The answer is that our first humanoid (symbolizing and conceptualizing) ancestors were very ignorant, but not at all stupid. They were ignorant of the laws of genetics, but they were smart enough to suspect that such laws exist. Sperm-egg fusion is surrounded by violent taboos and fierce tribal conformity because the survival and future evolution of the gene pool depends upon *which* particular spermatozoa reaches *which* particular ovum.

Etymologists confirm the Freudian theory that there are ancient linkages between the words for the sacred, the erotic, the obscene, the awe inspiring, the aw-ful, the divine, the "thrilling." All of these are primitive, powerful *physiological* responses to the mysteries of *sexual attraction, mating, reproduction, inheritance, genetic drift, future evolution.* The earliest god-forms found by archeologists are pregnant goddesses and ithyphallic gods. The most intolerant, bigoted and recalcitrant of all prejudices -- the very last to fade away after cosmopolitanizing contact with other tribes having different values -- are the taboos concerning *the right to reproduce.* If one nation insists that the head of state must marry his sister, and another insists that he must not, both are acting on the assumption that *the right way* must be found and rigorously enforced.

There are unknowns in the area of *sexual attraction* -- He likes Her, but She doesn't like Him.

There are unknowns in the area of *mating* -- a young couple can make love once, and the woman becomes pregnant, yet another couple make love for three years and the woman remains barren. Very puzzling and frightening for primitives, in New Guinea or New Jersey.

**GODS AND GODDESSES ARE SEXUAL AND GENETIC
PROGRAMS EXPRESSED IN PRIMITIVE SYMBOLS.**

There are unknowns in the area of *reproduction* -- why twins? Why three boys in one family and three girls in another? Why miscarriages and stillbirths?

There are unknowns in the area of *inheritance* -- "Why doesn't my son look like me?" many a domesticated primate has wondered uneasily, leading to a great deal of paranoia and male chauvinism.

There are unknowns in the area of *genetic drift* -- modern researchers recognize twelve or more variables, but still have more questions than answers.

There are unknowns in the area of *future evolution* -- "Where do we come from, what are we, where are we going?", the title of Gauguin's greatest painting, is the basic ontological question; the totem-pole, like the treatise on sociobiology, is an attempt to answer.

Amid all these unknowns -- of sexual attraction, mating reproduction, inheritance, genetic drift, future evolution -- the shamans of every tribe try to establish guide-posts to tribal (gene-pool) survival.

Thus "morality" is invented.

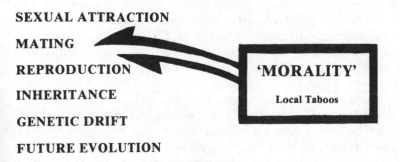

SEXUAL ATTRACTION

MATING

REPRODUCTION

INHERITANCE

GENETIC DRIFT

FUTURE EVOLUTION

'MORALITY'

Local Taboos

Sexual attraction, mating, reproduction, inheritance, genetic drift and future evolution are all *stochastic* processes. (That is, processes in which, out of a random series, some "intelligence" or something that can be metaphorically conceived as an intelligence, is selecting a final outcome.) That these stochastic processes overlap, as shown in our diagram, is intuitively obvious; and it is also obvious that the future is being "selected" every step of the way.* Taboo and morality are tribal attempts to govern the random element -- to select the desired future.

"Morality" attempts to control the stochastic evolutionary process at two points -- interfering between sexual attraction and sexual consumation (Mating) by taboos and commandments, or else interfering between mating and reproduction. The latter case is represented by infanticide a widespread birth-control measure always justified by the local shamans on magical grounds, e.g. the infants selected for sacrifice are breach births, or birth-marked, or twins, or in some way stigmatized by the "gods." The actual function of such practices, of course, is population control; and such customs are most common on isolated islands where runaway population would be a disaster. Similarly, the Judaic taboos functioned to channel all sexuality into increased population, since the ancient Jews were surrounded by large and pugnacious Empires eager to conquer them; they needed more boys for soldiers and more girls to breed soldiers.

The most "idiotic" and "superstitious" taboos, from the Rationalist viewpoint, always had *some* function when invented. For instance, the most "pointlessly" elaborate (non-genetic) "incest" taboos, in which virtually everybody in the tribe becomes unavailable sexually to everybody else, force *exogamy* (marriage outside the tribe). This creates affectional alliances (family ties) between tribes and decreases warfare. Something like this primitive exogamy survived into very recent times, in the custom of marrying one royal family to another.

Every form of "morality" is, of course, irksome on some level to everybody, because no individual ever has *exactly* the sexual imprint desired by the tribe. The more sophisticated totem-cults (the "higher" religions, so dubbed by themselves) take account of this by the doctrine of atonement. In one form or another, this allows the individual to be ritually "Forgiven" periodically for not being the perfect sexual robot decreed by tribal morality.

---

*That the whole chain is "intelligent" or manifests "intelligence," is the Lamarckian heresy which Darwinians have never quite been able to kill; everytime it is buried, it rises again in new form. Two most able recent arguments of the neo-Lamarckian or meta-Lamarckian postion, which the reader is cordially urged to read, are Timothy Leary's *The Intelligence Agents* and Gregory Bateson's *Mind and Nature*.

This becomes hilarious only when one realizes that most of what domesticated primates are asking their priests to forgive them for consists of what Kinsey so accurately called "normal mammalian behavior."*

*This only refers to the silly and inferior religions of other people, of course, and has no reference to the Sublime Truths of the reader's own religion.

109

Time-binding (the transmission of symbols and tools across generations) begins on the third circuit. Acute *consciousness of time* is, however, intensified on the fourth circuit.

The principle function of the socio-sexual circuit, in the higher primates, is to form an *adult personality* -- a parent.* By definition, the parent is one who cares for the young of the species; by genetic necessity, the parent also cares *about* the young. In symbolizing humans, this means planning, hoping and having aspirations. In the language of the mystics, this means being "attached" and "trapped on the wheel of karma"; the first effort in most mystical traditions is to break this fourth-circuit attachment by taking a vow of celibacy.

The fourth circuit is located in the *left neo-cortex* -- the newest part of the left hemisphere of the brain. It is linked neurologically with the *genitalia* and the *breasts* (fucking-hugging-embracing-protecting circuitry).

Persons who take their heaviest imprint on this circuit are *beautiful.* That is, their entire body has received so many sexual neurotransmitters from the brain that they are constantly radiating the "attractive" *mating signals* that make up our perception of what is "beautiful" in a human being.

According to accidents of imprinting, they *can be* coldly calculating exploiters, totally repressed Puritans or carry some other negative traits but they always *look like* (send the signals of) the ideal fucker-lover-protector.

Once formulated, "morality" serves as not only a check on genetic drift but a brake against Circuit III innovation. The shamans, priests etc. *define* which ideas are "moral" and which are "immoral." Anything new -- anything that will break the

---

*Homosexuality (like left-handedness) is probably included in the genetic script to serve auxiliary functions. In most primitive societies, the homosexuals (and the left-handed) are shunted into shamanic roles. In more complex societies they are (like spinsters and heterosexual bachelors) usually shunted into intellectual or artistic roles, which have quasi-shamanic functions of making, breaking or transforming cultural signals. Those who claim any perennial sexual variation is "against nature" are underestimating nature's variety, diversity and economy. The "mutation" of Leonardo de Vinci, a left-handed homosexual, was needed to break up the signal of the dying medieval reality-tunnel and remake our perceptions into the reality-tunnel of post-Renaissance scientific humanism. His success is registered by the fact that a Leonardo painting is still the "norm" of what we mean by realism, i.e. most people (including right-handed heterosexuals) are living in the scientific-humanist "space" this man invented.

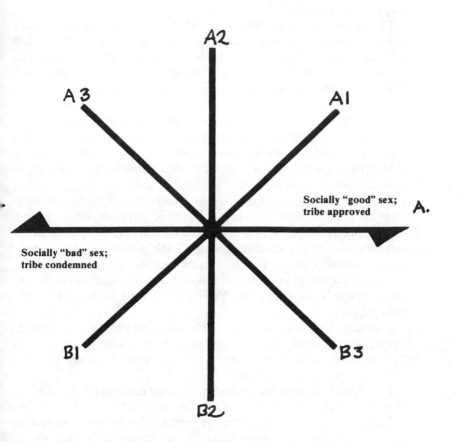

IMPRINTING THE SOCIO-SEXUAL CIRCUIT

A and B represent socially "good" and socially "bad" sex, according to the tribe. A1, A2, and A3 represent individual imprints -- personally "good" sex (what the individual is imprinted to like) -- and B1, B2 and B3 personally "bad" (what the individual doesn't like). If Axis A1-B1 is only slightly tilted, the individual is fairly "normal" (in that society). If A2-B2 is tilted more; the individual is "neurotic" (in that society). If A3-B3 is tilted much further; the individual is a "pervert" (in that society).

tribal cycle, i.e. take us out of cyclical mythic "time" into linear, progressive, revolutionary "time" -- is usually defined, very quickly, as "immoral."

To say that religion and priestcraft have played a conservative role in history is an understatement. One might as well say that bubonic plague has killed a few people, or that Hitler was a little bit strange. *The chief role of religion has always been reactionary.* This is its evolutionary function, in the dialectic of the circuitry of the brain.

Circuit III, unchecked, is like a cocaine monologue. You can't remember anything, because everything is changing too fast. This is profoundly disorienting to the average domesticated primate, so the tribal moralists keep stability and tranquility by acting as decelerators,

The average person, similarly, is philosophically most "open" and "curious" *before* the adult sex role of parenthood is elected. *After* reproduction, there is little time for Circuit III speculations, and (because of the sanctions every tribe places upon "heresy," i.e. new ideas) there is also little inclination.

Thus, Circuit III tends to take us out of tribal cyclical time into linear progressive time; but Circuit IV loops us back into the cycle again.

Homosexuals may or may not be the chief creators of cultural innovation, as some Gay Pride advocates claim; but it is certainly true that they have done more than their share. The reason? They are not trapped into parent roles.

These four circuits are coded, with four permutations of each, into the "court cards" of the Tarot deck.

Thus the Knight of Discs, representing earth/earth according to the occultists, is the pure First Circuit type -- all sensation, all oral demand, all viscerotonic. Behind their alchemical, Cabalistic, theosophical jargon, most books on Tarot are describing this type when they discuss this card. The pure undiluted "Momma's boy."

The Queen of Discs, or earth/water, is a mixture of first and second circuit traits -- sensational-viscerotonic-oral and emotional-egotistic-political. You better be damned careful to call her Ms.

The Prince of Discs, or earth/air, is a blend of first and third circuits -- oral demand and rational calculation. Probably, a very sharp and sharkish lawyer.

The Princess of Discs, or earth/fire is first circuit orality mixed with fourth circuit sexuality. This fusion of exhibitionism with enflamed eros means she's probably starring in porn movies. In all Disc cards, the first circuit predominates over the others.

The Queen of Cups, or water/water, is emotion and territorial demand. Nelson Algren had her in mind when he said, "Never bed down with a woman who has more problems than you."

The Knight of Cups, water/earth, is emotion plus sensation. The pure predator, marauder, thief, rapist or sociopath.

The Prince of Cups or water/air is emotion plus reason. The humanist, humanitarian, liberal; an ideal Unitarian minister.

The Princess of Cups is water/fire: an explosive mixture of egotism and sexuality. Scarlett O'Hara. The *femme fatale*.

The Prince of Swords is air/air: all pure undiluted intellect. His feet never touch the earth; he lives amid floating abstractions. The monk-scholar.

The Knight of Swords is air/earth: reason and oral exhibitionism. The actor, orator, demagogue -- sometimes the artist.

The Queen of Swords is air/water; reason plus emotion. The greats in science and art are generally of this imprint group.

The Princess of Swords is air/fire: reason and sexuality. The good parent; usually the Puritan, but sometimes the crusader for "sexual freedom." In any case, the motivating drive is an attempt to impose abstract reason upon the genetic imperatives of the mating urge.

The Princess of Wands is fire/fire: sexuality at its most powerful. These types are usually, but not necessarily, quite promiscuous; sometimes they pour all their erotic energy into one mate and raise huge families, parenting being a strong part of the fourth circuit; e.g. J. S. Bach, who may have written the sexiest music in history, had twenty children.

The Knight of Wands is fire/earth: sexuality and sensationalism. The Playboy. Reich's "Phallic Narcissist."

The Prince of Wands is fire/air: sexuality plus reason. These types are likely to get involved in the kind of empirical mysticism that is *not* tolerated by the local Authorities -- e.g. the Tantrists in India, the Knights Templar and witches in medieval Europe, Aleister Crowley and Wilhelm Reich most recently. (Crowley said this card was a portrait of his "True Self.")

The Queen of Wands is fire/water: sexuality and emotional

113

politics. The law courts have a steady parade of this type passing through every day.

The clever Cabalists who designed this pictoral key to the four primitive circuits included a clue to higher consciousness. For they teach that each element in traditional alchemy (earth, air, fire, water) corresponds to one of these Tarot suits (discs, swords, wands, cups) and to one of the letters in the Holy Unspeakable Name of God -- YHVH. The correspondences are as follows:

Y	fire	wands	CIRCUIT IV
H	water	cups	CIRCUIT II
V	air	swords	CIRCUIT III
H	earth	discs	CIRCUIT I

The logic of this imagery is quite clear to the unconscious mind, and these associations appear frequently in dreams, as Jung documented in PSYCHOLOGY AND ALCHEMY.

| Knight of Wands | Queen of Cups | Prince of Swords | Princess of Discs |

CIRCUIT I	CIRCUIT II	CIRCUIT III	CIRCUIT IV
Oral narcissist sensation	Emotionalist feeling	Rationalist reason	Sex Role
Natural Child	Adapted Child	Adult or Computer	(missing in Jung)
Id	Ego	(missing in Freud)	Parent
			Super-ego

The aim of the Cabala is to make "the microcosm mirror the macrocosm"; that is, to make the human being a perfect image of "God." This means putting together the four "alchemical" elements symbolized by the letters Y,H,V,H. In other words, bringing the four circuits into balance.

This is the same lesson as taught in the Buddhist mandalas with four demons at the corners and the circle representing awakening in the middle.

The "married look,"the "Mom and Dad look," etc., which are not scientific concepts but which everybody can recognize at once, have to do with an acute *time-sense*. The parent is concerned not just with acquiring bio-survival tickets for personal nurture, but with acquiring tickets for the young, and for the future.

Behaviorists tell us wonderful stories about the intricate patterns that can be conditioned into experimental animals. See they say we have, by selective reinforcement, trained this rat so that at the sound of a bell, he runs up a ladder, presses button A, races across a plank and down another ladder, presses button B, dashes across the cage and waits at the food-slot for his meal to arrive.

Lest anybody think this book is written from a perch of superiority, consider the similar, but more complex, behavior which the author followed for twenty years. He would set an alarm clock before sleep every night. When the alarm woke him, he would breakfast hurriedly, rush off to catch a bus, ride to a subway, change to the train, ride to an office building, rush through the lobby, board an elevator, ride to a certain floor, enter an office, and toil at repetitious (and generally pointless) tasks for eight hours. This behavior sequence had been shaped, as B.F. Skinner would say, by reinforcement delivered every second week in the form of bio-survival tickets (money). These tickets were necessary to the bio-survival of four dependent children.

The reader of this book can probably remember, somewhat dimly, the imprinting and conditioning of each of these circuits.

We all began as infants in a one-dimensional world, orally hooked to Mommy. The further away from Mommy we crawled, the greater was our bio-survival anxiety, and we generally returned to Mommy as quickly as possible. The key imprint incidents of this period, together with associated conditioning, determine, concretely, how much we presently exhibit of:

ANXIETY	OR	SELF-CONFIDENCE
ROOTEDNESS	OR	EXPLORATIVENESS
DEPENDENCY	OR	INDEPENDENCE

Then, when the DNA sent the appropriate RNA messenger molecules to the glands, endocrine system, etc. a *mutation* occurred. Our gross morphology -- our whole body -- changed, and our "minds" changed in the process. That is, our reality-tunnel dilated into two-dimensions, when we *rose up* and began to *walk* about the house, and started learning who we could dominate, who could dominate us, who could be dominated (emotionally bullied) at some times and not at others, etc. We developed out of amorphous bio-survival *consciousness* into stubborn individual *ego*. We were imprinted and conditioned with a particular style of emotional-territorial "politics."

At this stage we were imprinted and conditioned for:

DOMINANCE	OR	SUBMISSION
SELF-CONFIDENCE	OR	SELF-DOUBT
STRONG EGO	OR	WEAK EGO
HIGH PACK STATUS	OR	LOW PACK STATUS
GIVING ORDERS	OR	TAKING ORDERS
"HERRENMORAL"	OR	"SKLAVMORAL"

We were subsequently conditioned to switch between these reflexes depending on whether the person we were dealing with was Higher in the pecking order or Lower in the pecking order. (Middle-class people, e.g. Reagan conservatives, John Birchers, etc. will *always* revere those Higher in the pecking order; and, equally, will always have some reason to persecute -- peck at -- the poor, who are Lower in the pecking order. Hence, they will say and even believe, that they are being robbed by the poor on Welfare -- who get about 4% of the tax dollar -- and never "notice" that the military-industrial complex is getting 72% of their tax dollar. This is normal mammalian sociobiology.)

After this second-circuit reality-tunnel is wired in, the organism molts and mutates again into the verbal stage, and a third circuit style of mentation is imprinted. That is, on top of protoplasmic consciousness and mammalian ego, we acquire human *mind,* which is created by and creator of human artifacts and speech. Feral children, who survived in isolation from human society (artifacts and speech), have no *"mind"* in the human sense; which is why they are called feral.

In the semantic stage of imprint vulnerability we acquire either:

FLUENCY	OR	INARTICULATENESS
DEXTERITY	OR	CLUMSINESS
"GOOD MIND"	OR	"DUMB MIND"*

At puberty, another DNA trigger fires and RNA messengers initiate another morphological mutation of body-mind. The "adult personality" is imprinted and conditioned. We become:

"MORAL"	OR	"IMMORAL"
ROBOT-OBEDIENT	OR	ROBOT-DISOBEDIENT
SOLID CITIZEN	OR	SEXUAL OUTLAW
"PARENT"	OR	ANARCHIST

Lack of understanding of these morphological changes, and their persistence in imprint circuits in the brain, is responsible for *most* failures in communication, and for the general sense of exasperation with which we too often confront each other. Since everybody's imprints are a little bit different -- *the average is that which nobody totally is*** -- we all feel at times like the legendary Quaker who told his wife, "All the world is mad but me and thee, and sometimes I wonder about thee."

Reichians, disciples of Dr. Spock and the Summerhill School, etc. have called attention, with some impatience, to the brutality and stupidity of many of our traditional child-rearing methods. These methods are "brutal" and "stupid" only if, like the above-mentioned heretics, one regards the goal of child-rearing as the production of a sane, balanced, creative **[NOT CRATED]**

---

*Why do we say "dumb" (mute) for *stupid?* Because "a good mind means a good mouth," and the human mind is a verbalizing circuit.
**James Joyce justified anarchism on the grounds that "the state is concentric and the individual is eccentric."

human being. **THIS HAS NEVER BEEN THE GOAL OF ANY SOCIETY IN THE REAL WORLD.** The traditional child-rearing methods are quite logical, pragmatic and sound in fulfilling the *real* purpose of society, which is *not* to create an ideal person, but to create **[CRATE]** a semi-robot who mimics the society as closely as possible -- both in its rational and its irrational aspects, both as the repository of the wisdom of the past and as the sum total of all the cruelties and stupidities of the past. Very simply, a totally aware, alert, *awakened* (unbrainwashed) person would not fit very well into any of the standard roles society offers; the damaged, robotized products of traditional child-rearing *do* fit into those slots.

That is, there is a neuro-sociological "logic" to the illogical. Are traditional schools very much like mini-prisons? Do they stifle imagination, cramp the child physically and mentally, and run on various forms of overt or covert terrorism? Of course, the answer is an unambiguous *yes;* but such schools are necessary to train people for roles in the ordinary office or factory or profession, which are also very much like mini-prisons, stifle imagination, cramp the person physically and mentally and run on terror (threat of loss of bio-survival tickets, in the form of pay-checks or tenure).

The permissive movement in child-rearing appeared only when it did, and has succeeded only to a limited extent, because society has always needed and still thinks it needs human robots. Utopian child-rearing will advance further, necessarily, only as society itself evolves out of authoritarianism. That is, as the accelerated changes now occurring propel us into the most rapid period of social evolution in all human history, we will then need citizens *who are not* robots, *who are* creative; *who are not* docile, *who are* innovative; *who are not* narrow-minded bigots, *who are* explorers in every sense of the word.

Traditional child-rearing began to falter only when society began to enter into the present period of accelerated change and technological omni-transformation of all traditional values.

Failures in communication generally derive from sending a message to the wrong address. That is, your husband has an *ego* problem and you send a message to his *mind.* Adapting a diagram from Transactional Analysis what has happened is this:

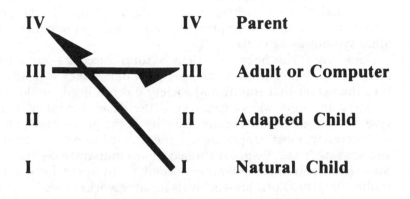

	IV	Parent
IV		
III	III	Adult or Computer
II	II	Adapted Child
I	I	Natural Child

The message is addressed from Circuit I to Circuit IV. It means "I feel weak; help bolster me up." If the answer comes back from Circuit III to Circuit III, "Well, let's analyze the problem . . ." there has been a Wrong Address.

Of course, this example is deliberately untypical, although not impossible. It is untypical because women traditionally are trained *not* to make this kind of mistake -- to be "emotionally sensitive," to be "supportive," etc. It is much more likely, statistically;, that this kind of Wrong Address will go the other way --husband to wife. That is, the wife signals "Help!" and the husband on Circuit III says, "Let's analyze the problem . . ."

We have said that the imprinting of the circuits contains a large element of accident (within genetic parameters). Society, everywhere, without understanding this theory, understands enough *pragmatically* about imprinting processes to attempt to program each individual for his or her assigned role. Hence, traditional girl-rearing is different from traditional boy-rearing, so that women *will* have more Circuit II "sensitivity." Again Women's Liberation, like modern child-rearing, arrived only when we were evolutionarily ready or nearly-ready for it. *The traditional system worked in traditional societies.*

Similarly, class structure, like the caste structure in an insect hive, works to produce the "right" imprints in each class. The third circuit of the servile class or proletariat is imprinted chiefly for manual dexterity, while the same circuit in middle-class or ruling-class children is imprinted for verbal, mathematical or other symbol-using skills

Democracy has been less than a total success -- and the intellectual's half-shamed cynicism about democracy is justified -- to the extent that traditional society did not need, could not use, and in many ways discouraged the development of high verbal ("rational") skills in the majority of the population. That is, concretely, most people are not encouraged to be very smart, and are rather heavily programmed to be comparatively stupid. Such programming is what is needed to fit them into most traditional jobs. Their bio-survival circuitry works as well as that of most animals, their emotional-territorial circuitry is typically primate, and they have little third circuit "mind" to verbalize (rationalize) with. Naturally, they usually vote for the charlatan who can activate primitive bio-survival fears and territorial ("patriotic") pugnacity. The intellectual looks at the dismal results and continues to believe in "democracy" only by an act of Blind Faith similar to the way beliefs in Catholicism or Communism or snake-worship are maintained.

Again, the traditional system *works,* for traditional society. A mass made of people who have intense curiosity about why Beethoven went in for string quartets after the Ninth Symphony, or whether Kant really refuted Hume satisfactorily, or what the latest quantum theories *mean* in relation to Determinism and Free Will, is not a mass that will easily be led into dull, dehumanizing labor at traditional jobs.

Why did Adlai Stevenson lose to Ike Eisenhower, George McGovern to Tricky Dicky Nixon, etc? It was the Wrong Address problem again. Stevenson, McGovern and other darlings of the intelligentsia were speaking to the third circuit, which is not very highly developed in most domesticated primates yet. Eisenhower in his Fatherly way, and Nixon in his bullying Big Brother way, knew just how to push the right Second Circuit emotional-territorial buttons to get a mob of primates to follow them. They were genetically programmed alpha males, in ethological terms.

Similarly, the Moralist (i.e. the Adult Personality who has imprinted heavy Ethical imperatives on Circuit IV) is often totally unable to communicate with the scientist or technologist. The Moralist may even decide -- many already have -- that the scientist *per se* is "inhuman." In fact, morals are fairly irrelevant to the Third Circuit analytical mind, which is the brain function the average scientist has imprinted most powerfully. To the third circuit, the only morality is accuracy, the only immorality is sloppy thinking.

Again, the rise in "social conscience" among scientists is happening only when it was evolutionarily necessary that it happen, i.e. after Hiroshima. If it doesn't seem to be happening widely enough and quickly enough, well, the same can be said -- also in error, I think -- about modernizing education and child-rearing, about Womens Liberation, about racism, etc. The rebellion against all the follies of the past is succeeding, and will continue to succeed, only as we evolve into a society which needs *each human to function well on all circuits.* We are moving with ever-increasing speed, into such a society.

What the impatient radical forgets is that many of the "injustices" of the traditional primate society were not even *perceived* as such by the best minds of 1000 years ago or 100 years ago, or in the case of institutionalized sexism, even 20 years ago. If we can see injustice and absurdity in many age-old institutions, it is only because we are evolving out of robothood, at precisely the point in evolution when it is necessary for us to become smarter and more sensitive on all circuits.

Each of us has a "favorite" circuit -- that is, a circuit that has been more heavily imprinted than the others. Miscommunication, misunderstanding and general misjudgement of one another is vastly increased by the fact that few of us know about these levels of circuitry, and *we all tend to assume that the person we are interacting with is on the same circuit we are.*

Thus, there are narcissistic (oral) first circuit types in every social group. Present them with a problem and they will immediately look for somebody else to handle it, since the oral stage is robotically imprinted for dependency. (Or, if they have imprinted hostile weakness instead of dependent weakness, they will explode into anger -- infantile tantrum -- raging that a problem exists and that it has been imposed on them.)

A second circuit type, in the same situation, will attempt to frighten the problem away by barking and blustering at it, mammalian-fashion.

A third circuit type will try to reason out the problem. This is the best approach *only* with problems that are themselves rational, i.e. "How do you make this machine work?" It can be blind, and futile, when the "problem" is another human being acting out one of the more destructive second-circuit rage programs.

("The liberal is the one who leaves the room when the fight starts," somebody once said. Third circuit types are most confused and feel impotent when second circuit mammalian politics takes over the scene.)

A fourth circuit type will try to be rational (third circuit) and to sense the emotional dimensions of the problem (second circuit) but will basically try to impose a *moral* solution: "Now this is the decent, fair thing to do . . ." This may or may not make sense to the third circuit Rationalist, looking for objective justice; and it will usually make no sense at all to the totally second-circuit type dominated by emotionalism and territoriality.

What is true of the group is true of the the individual. While we all have our favorite circuit, and tend to see that circuit as "superior" to all the others, we can be pushed out of it by shocks or stresses, in which case we jump to another circuit.

The most robotic Rationalist will descend to the first circuit, eventually, if threat to bio-security is forcibly enough presented on the screen of consciousness. And, if prevented from "leaving the room when the fight starts," the Rationalist will even descend to second-circuit mammalian howling and barking, under sufficient pressure. (Oliver Wendell Holmes referred to this as "the hydrostatic principle in controversy," whereby the fools drag everybody down to their own level.)

The most robotic Emotionalist may also move up to the third

circuit, temporarily, if a problem remains intractable to every form of emotional bullying or con-artistry.

All of us will move into fourth circuit Parent role or Super Ego -- even little children will do it, imitatively -- if it seems that the only way to get what one wants is to appeal to tribal morality: "Why, it would be *positively indecent* not to do it the way Grandfather would . . ."

"Give us the child until he is five, and we will have him for life," bragged some 18th Century Jesuit. The Jesuit order of that time, as Aldous Huxley later noted sardonically, educated Voltaire, Diderot, and the Marquis de Sade; obviously their techniques of brain-programming were not perfect. Nonetheless, most people in most societies do grow up as fairly accurate replicas of the previous generation. Most children educated by the Jesuits have remained Catholics. Most children of Democrats do *not* become Republicans. Etc.

Considering the wide variety of philosophies available to any of us -- nudism and Buddhism, scientific materialism and snake-worship, Communism and vegetarianism, subjective Idealism and existentialism, Methodism and Shinto, etc. -- the fact that most people remain in the same reality-tunnel as their parents, does indicate that acculturalization is a mind control process. We are all giants, raised by pygmies, who have learned to walk with a perpetual mental crouch. Unleashing our full stature -- our total brain power -- is what this book is all about.

There is a Zen story (very funny -- ha-ha) about a monk who, having failed to achieve "enlightenment" (brain-change) through the normal Zen methods, was told by his teacher to think of nothing but an ox. Day after day after day, the monk thought of the ox, visualized the ox, meditated on the ox. Finally, one day, the teacher came to the monk's cell and said, "Come out here -- I want to talk to you."

"I can't get out," the monk said. "My horns won't fit through the door."

I can't get out . . .

At these words, the monk was "enlightened." Never mind what "enlightenment" means, right now. The monk went through some species of brain change, obviously. He had developed the delusion that he *was* an ox, and awakening from that hypnoidal state he saw through the mechanism of all other delusions and how they robotize us.

EXERCIZES

1. Recreate *vividly* in imagination your first orgasm. To what extent do you still use the same accessories (stimuli) to turn you on?

2. Try to change your sexual imprint. See if you can reach orgasm by some method that has been taboo or unthinkable to you before.

3. Imagine that you are Rev. Jerry Falwell. Explain to an imaginary homosexual why his sexual imprint is "sinful" and should be changed at once. Include instructions on how to change it.

4. Imagine that you are a Gay man or Lesbian. Explain to Rev. Falwell why you will not or can not change your sexual imprint to please him.

5. Read Margaret Mead's *Sex and Temperament in Three Primitive Societies.* Then write a five-page proof that the taboos in our tribe make more sense objectively than the taboos of the tribes she studied. *Be serious about it!*

6. Choose the viewpoint of the Samoans in Dr. Mead's book above. Write a five-page proof that their taboos make more sense than those of our society. Be serious about it.

7. Re-read the paragraphs about the giraffe and the gosling. What does this tell you about your sexual imprint? What is your jeep or your ping-pong ball?

CHAPTER NINE

MINDWASHING AND BRAIN PROGRAMMING

We have certain preconceived notions about
location in space which have come down to us
from ape-like ancestors.

Sir Arthur Eddington,
Space, Time and Gravitation

The greatest Utopian possibility before us is also the greatest dystopian terror.

We are learning more and more about the pragmatics of *brain change:* how to alter anybody's brain so as to set them in a totally new "reality." Visions of *1984* and *Brave New World* lurk in this very concept.

But we are also learning how to change our own brains -- learning to use them for fun and profit rather than for misery and robothood. Visions of Super-Humanity are implicit in any perception of what this means.

The brain can be tuned, like a TV, to turn off any channel, and to bring in a new channel. This is what the veterans of the 1960s-1970s Neurological Revolution know. This is the major threat, and the major promise of our time.

Consider the alternatives.

CYANIDE AND SYNCHRONICITY

In November 1978, I was in Seattle to see the 10-hour play which Ken Campbell had made out of the three *Illuminatus!* novels by Bob Shea and myself. In the course of the drama came a scene Shea and I had almost forgotten writing in the seven years since the books were finished in 1971. The scene concerned a lunatic messiah who orders 3300 of his robot disciples to commit suicide by drinking cyanide. The mindless automatons obey and each drinks his cyanide cocktail.

Shea and I had written that bizarre sequence to illustrate the extremes to which brainwashing can go. We both regarded it as an extravagant fantasy, for satirical purposes -- an exaggeration of our serious theme.

Yet while the actors on the stage were depicting this "fantasy" every TV and newspaper in the land was discussing the exact same species of mass zombie behavior. Our fictional maniac-guru was Adolph Hitler; in November 1978, while our play was being performed, another maniac-guru, Jim Jones, had played the whole sequence out in reality. In Guyana, he had ordered 900 of his robots to drink cyanide and they had all obeyed.

It was particularly interesting to me that Jones had staged his *Gotterdammerung* while our play was having its American premiere. It was even more interesting that the tool of mass suicide, in our fiction and in Jones's reality, had been cyanide.

Carl Jung, the psychologist, and Wolfgang Pauli, the physicist, had a name for peculiar coincidences of that order of eeriness. They called them *synchronicities* and said they represented an acausal and/or holistic principle in nature that acts outside the linear past-present-future of Newtonian time.

Pauli, like most quantum physicists, was aware that sub-atomic events cannot be understood in Newtonian terms and must require some sort of acausality (*indeterminism*) or holism (*super-determinism*) to explain them. *In either case, the distinction between "observer" and "observed" breaks down.* (About that, more later.)

Jung, in turn, had observed that such synchronicities -- weird coincidences -- tend to occur when certain deep structures in the psyche are activated. He assumed that these structures were at what he called "the psychoid level," *below* the collective unconscious, where mind and matter are not yet distinct -- the quantum foam out of which matter and form and consciousness hierarchically emerge.

Wait. It gets weirder . . .

HEIRESS TO BANK ROBBER

When Patty Hearst was kidnapped by the Symbionese Liberation Army on February 4, 1974, she was a "normal" young heiress. She was attending a normal college, had a normal live-in boy-friend and smoked a normal amount of weed for a young heiress of that time. 57 days later, she had become a new person, with a new name -- Tania -- and was living in a new reality-tunnel.

Where Patty had been heterosexual, Tania was bisexual. Where Patty largely accepted the Hearst family tunnel-reality with only a few "liberal" modifications typical of her age group, Tania was a violent and fanatic revolutionary. Where Patty had been respectful to her parents, Tania denounced them as "corporate liars" and castigated them as being involved in a capitalist plot to "murder" the poor people of the U.S. "down to the last man, woman and child." Where Patty had been "nice" and polite and certainly non-violent, Tania had her photo taken holding a tommy-gun and assisted in at least one bank robbery and perhaps other felonies.

What had happened? When Patty-Tania was captured and brought to trial, the defense claimed that she had been "brainwashed." The jury either did not understand or did not believe this; they sentenced Patty to prison for the crimes Tania had committed. Debate about this case continues to the present, since some people think Ms. Hearst was "responsible" for the consciousness change she underwent while held captive by the SLA and others are just as sure she was not "responsible."

Leaving metaphysical questions of "responsibility" aside for a moment, it seems obvious that a young lady of Hearst's class and background would almost certainly not have taken up bankrobbing if she had not first been kidnapped and incorporated by the SLA.

Since the SLA called itself an army, let us compare it to an army; this may prove illuminating.

One does not get kidnapped into an army the way Hearst got kidnapped into the SLA, but the process is not entirely dissimilar. U.S. Army recruiters do not break into a young man's house in the middle of night with guns, as the SLA did with Patty: they simply send the young man a notice in the mail. Nonetheless *coercion* is there; the young draftee knows that if he ignores the letter, government agents will be around to seize his body in a short while, (unless he flees the country.) He will then either go into the army or into jail. Thus, whether we are speaking about the S.L. Army or the U.S. Army, the subject is reduced to infantile helplessness: other people are deciding what is to be done to his or her body. One is pushed to the neonate position of being one foot high in a six foot tall world, as it were. Like the small child, one is learning that the first rule of survival is to obey.

Most people (except nudists) are shy about appearing naked in public -- and this is the most common of all nightmares, "There I was with no clothes on!" (Joyce made this the central incident in the dream that is all dreams, *Finnegans Wake*.) The first step in leaving the civilian reality-tunnel and being initiated into the Army reality-tunnel is, thus, the physical examination, in which the subject is stripped naked and made to march around a large building with other naked victims while the fully-clothed Army personnel give the briefest possible orders: "Stand up. Sit down. Go there. Come back here," etc. The Masonic initiation, which only removes part of the clothing of the subject, is a milder version of the *stripping* away of previously secure social parameters.

What is really being "stripped away" is more subtle; it is the whole social system in which one has lived before being snatched by a U.S. or an S.L. Army. When the doctor tells the naked draftee, "Bend over. Spread your cheeks," so-called normal reality has ended as totally as if the victim had been incorporated into a surrealist movie. If an employer becomes too obnoxious, one can always find a new job. You cannot walk out on the U.S. or S.L. Army that way, because acute first-circuit helplessness is being imprinted.

When the Russian mathematician, Ouspensky, was first studying with Gurdjieff, he had great trouble understanding Gurdjieff's insistence that most people are machines and totally unaware of the objective world around them. Then, one day, after World War I had begun, Ouspensky saw a truck full of *artificial legs*. These artificial legs were being sent to the front-line hospitals, for soldiers whose legs had not even been blown off yet, but whose legs *would* be blown off. The prediction that these legs would be blown off was so certain that the artificial legs were already on their way to replace the natural legs. The prediction was based on the mathematical certainty that millions of young men would march to the front, to be maimed and murdered, as mindlessly as cattle marching into a slaughterhouse.

In a flash, Ouspensky understood the *mechanical* nature of ordinary human consciousness.

("I can't get out -- my horns won't fit through the door.")

Initiation into the "Manson family" is not dissimilar. Lynette Fromme was much like Patty Hearst -- a "normal" American young woman, with less money than Hearst, but no special proclivity for criminal behavior. After passing through General Manson's basic training, Lynette had become Squeaky Fromme and was convicted for pointing a gun at the U.S. President with seeming intent to assassinate him.

In the next chapter we will explain further how being captured ("drafted") by an army is the model of all brainwashing experience.

Human society as a whole is a vast brainwashing machine whose semantic rules and sex roles create a social robot.

The concept of washing" is, of course, unscientific and crude. The brain is not a dirty garment but an electro-colloidal information-tion processor -- a living network of over 110 billion nerve cells capable of ($10^{2783000}$) interconnections, a number higher than the total of all the atoms in the universe. In this elegant, microminiaturized biocomputer more than 100,000,000 processes are programmed every minute.

From the viewpoint of neuro-sociology, how I perceive "myself" and "my world" depends on how each circuit has been wired in my brain. Society has always known how to wire children; the process is called acculturalization; it explains why children of Catholics tend to become Catholics, children of Samoans fit into Samoan society, children of Russian Communists become good little Russian Communists, etc. Each generation "brainwashes" the next.

Christianity, Buddhism and Islam, between them, are the most potent brain-programming institutions on this planet. Approximately half the art and philosophy of the human race -- the architecture, the music, the paintings, the literature, the educational ideals, the "great ideas" -- has been influenced by and/or nurtured by these three great systems of theology. This is not to denigrate the contributions of Confucianism, Judaism, Hinduism, modern science, etc., but merely to emphasize the extent to which the higher civilizations have been shaped by the four creators of these three omni-religions: Buddha, Mohammed, Jesus and St. Paul. What did these four men have in common?

As Aleister Crowley points out, "No point of doctrine, no point of ethics, no theory of a 'hereafter' do they share, and yet in the history of their lives we find one identity amid many diversities."

Buddha was an ordinary Hindu nobleman, and then he experienced a rapid brain-change, after which he became a great Teacher.

Mohammed was a humble camel-driver, with no sign of exceptional intelligence or ambition, and then he experienced a rapid brain change, after which he became Teacher, Conqueror, Law-Maker and Prophet.

We hear nothing of Jesus (save a few fables) until the age of 30, when he experiences a rapid brain-change, and puts forth a doctrine that is to overturn the Roman Empire and influence Western Civilization until the present.

St. Paul, who took the teaching of Jesus and turned it into a militant movement, suffered an extreme form of brain-change, of which he tells us that he was temporarily struck blind and lifted up into the heavens where he beheld things "of which it is not lawful to speak."

On all else but the experience of Illumination they disagree. Buddha insisted that his enlightenment was perfectly natural --

"Are you a God?" he was once asked.

"No."

"Are you a saint?"

"No."

"Then what are you?"

"I am awake."

Mohammed informs us that he "spoke" to the Angel Gabriel, Jesus that the "Father which is in heaven" spoke *through* him, and St. Paul that he saw the lights and wonders above mentioned.

Making every possible reservation about fable and myth, we get this one coincidence: A nobody experiences rapid brain-change (consciousness dilation) and abruptly becomes very much a historical Somebody. Much of the human race is still living on the legacy of these four bio-electrical "illuminations," for good and for ill.

Most people (the present author included) would consider what happened to Patty Hearst "bad" and what happened to Buddha "good." It needs to be emphasized that both the "bad" and the "good" brain change experiences are functionally the same. The process is modelled, on a small scale by any design such as the following:

If you have seen this only one way, look at it again. There are two opposite ways of seeing it.

When your whole world, not just a design on a book-page, is transformed this way, you are experiencing the kind of brain-change that can turn a rich heiress into a bank robber, an obscure carpenter into a Messiah, or an ordinary bank teller into a mental patient . . .

Similar forms of major brain-change underlie all revolutionary break throughs in the arts, and in science as well. Neuro-sociology is a history of massive brain changes, as we quantum-jumped from "tribal" reality to "feudal" reality, from "feudal" reality to "industrial" reality, and now are jumping to Future Reality.

Consider the revolution against death, if you think *you* haven't been brainwashed.

Not all people have accepted mortality. Mystics, of course, have always insisted there is a species of "spiritual" immortality, but aside from that, Taoists in China and alchemists in Europe spent hundreds of years seeking the elixir of life that would allow for physical immortality. Paracelsus, for instance, left behind some of his sperm with directions to a student on how to revive or recreate him out of it. (He seems to have had a crude and inaccurate idea of cloning.) In the 1780s, both Benjamin Franklin and Condorcet, in America and France, wrote that medical science would eventually conquer death along with every other disease.

The modern immortalist movement began with physicist R.C.W. Ettinger who published *The Prospect of Immortality* in 1964. Ettinger, who had entered a reality-tunnel different from the imprinted consensus-reality of our tribe, said bluntly that we *could* be the generation that abolished death and we should start working for that goal.

Since then, research on life-extension and longevity has quantum jumped rapidly. Numerous books have come forth carrying the same basic message as Ettinger's. Among them have been:

The Biological Time Bomb, Taylor, 1968
The Immortalist, Harrington, 1969
The Immortality Factor, Segerberg, 1973
Here Comes Immortality, Tucille, 1974
Prolongevity, Rosenfeld, 1976
No More Dying, Kurtzman, 1978
The Life Extension Revolution, Kent, 1980

Dozens of societies have been founded for anti-aging research, to lobby for more research, or just to publicize the possibility before us -- the enormous evolutionary jump from mortality to immortality. Among these groups are: Committee for the Elimination of Death, San Marcos, Ca.; Bay Area Cryonics Society, San Francisco, Ca.; Prometheus Society, Baltimore, Md.; Long Life, Chicago, Ill.; Alcor Foundation, San Diego, Ca.; Foundation for Research Against Disease and Death, New York, N.Y. etc.

Now consider the cover of a recent book on this topic: *Conquest of Death* Alvin Silverstein, Ph.D. The front jacket says, in bold type but timid words:

A Controversial Look at the Revolution in Medicine and Why we May Be the Last Generation to Die

Note the pessimistic implications: immortality is coming, but not for me and you. *We* are still condemned to death. Our horns won't fit through the door.

This fatalistic version of Dr. Silverstein's message must have seemed necessary to the publishers because they felt that saying *we don't have to die* would be too shocking to the ordinary reader. What? You and I live forever? Nonsense! Our reality-tunnels have all been imprinted to end with the dying of the light.

Inside the jacket, a more accurate version of what Dr. Silverstein is saying appears:

We Need Not Be the Last Generation to Die -- We Can Conquer Death in our Time

Evidently, putting this on the front of the book would have been too much of a "Neurological Revolution" for the average reader -- at least in the publishers' estimation.

One has to reach page 189 of the book to find Dr. Silverstein's own estimate of the probable chronology of immortality, which is:

GOOD NEWS FOLKS

c. 1983 We begin to halt the aging process
c. 1989 Lifespan prolonged indefinitely
c. 1999 Conquest of disease and death

Are you ready for that possibility, or has your consciousness been so programmed that you cannot even think of it?

Who told you that you had to die? Were they any more infallible than the people who programmed Patty Hearst, etc.?

"But -- but -- the Immortalists are only a minority . . ." *(So were the Einsteinians in 1910.)*

"But -- but -- Reverend Jones told me to drink the cyanide and he knows what's right . . ."

"But -- but my horns won't fit through the door. . . "

EXERCIZES

1. Imagine yourself into the reality-tunnel of the far-right group known as the Minute Men. Believe for a while that the U.S. government is 85% under covert Communist control and an open Communist dictatorship will be declared soon. Turn on the TV in that frame of mind and *look for all the evidence* that each newscaster is either a conscious or an unconscious dupe of the Communist conspiracy.

2. Imagine yourself into the Head Space of a dogmatic Rationalist. Analyze the Jim Jones-cyanide-*Illuminatus* synchronicity as "mere coincidence."

3. Imagine yourself into the Head Space of an occultist. Analyze the Jim-Jones-cyanide-*Illuminatus* synchronicity as an Omen. What does it mean? Jungians say synchronicities contain "messages" from the deep structure of the collective mind. *What is the message?*

4. Enter the Immortalist head-space for a few minutes. Imagine you invest only $1000 at normal bank interest, compounded annually. What will you have in 100 years? In 200 years? (Nobody has used this conservative path to investment and gotten rich on it before because nobody has lived long enough.)

5. Why are you not a nudist (if you aren't)? Make up five good reasons, then go find a nudist and explain them to her (or him).

6. Become a Nazi for thirty three minutes. Believe that all politics is a matter of strength, stealth and treachery: that all liberalism is hypocrisy or folly. Plan a campaign to take over the world by force and fraud.

7. Go to a Fundamentalist revival meeting where faith-healings are performed. Or watch Jerry Falwell on T.V. Remember all the time that Jim Jones started out with that routine. See if you can get into the head space of the Believers and decide whether or not they would drink cyanide if their HOLY MAN told them to.

CHAPTER TEN

HOW TO BRAIN-WASH FRIENDS AND ROBOTIZE PEOPLE

There is no government, no industrial-military complex, no economic system, no mass media that can ever reduce us to puppets and robots as thoroughly as the biological and environmental dictatorships have.

F.M. Esfandiary, Upwingers

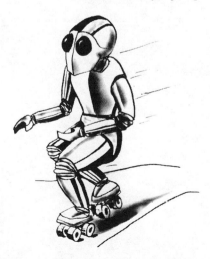

As noted earlier, when the bio-survival circuit flashes danger, *all other mental activity ceases.*

There is no "time" on the bio-survival circuit; reflexes act without emotional ego, rational mind or adult personality participating: "I just found myself doing it."

All the martial arts -- judo, akido, kung fu etc. -- are re-imprinting techniques for the bio-survival circuit. They are intended to ensure that *what happens mechanically* ("without thought") really does serve bio-survival, since the reflexes imprinted accidentally on this circuit are not that dependable.

The mechanical nature of the bio-survival circuit is of key importance in brainwashing. *To create a new imprint, reduce the victim to an infantile state, i.e. first circuit vulnerability.*

As pointed out in the last chapter an army begins this process with the draft notice, which informs the subject that his body no longer belongs to him but to the government. The S.L. Army, seeking quicker brain change, began the conversion of Patty into Tania by taking her at gun point, but the message was the same: "We can do what we want with your body from now on." First-circuit bio-survival instincts thus become hooked to obeying those who have this awesome power -- just as the infant learns to hook its bio-survival circuitry to the parental figures.

Patty's ride in the trunk of a car (after being taken at gun-point) is a classic rebirth ritual; the trunk is even womb-like in its contours. When the trunk opened, she was reborn into a new reality-tunnel, that of her captors. Similarly, where the earliest forms of masonic initiation survive and have not been diluted (Note the Adeptus Major Ritual in the *Complete Golden Dawn System of Magic*, by Israel Regardie, Falcon Press 1983.) the candidate is thrown into a well, and then "raised" as a newborn Freemason. *Total submersion*, the form of baptism preferred by Protestant fundamentalists, imitates this, but without the real anxiety that made traditional masonry and the S.L.A. so effective as brain change agents.

All brainwashers empirically know (without in most cases ever having read Leary's 8-circuit model of the brain) that the oral bio-survival circuit seeks bonding with a mothering figure. To increase panic and imprint vulnerability, then, the subject, after being seized by the brainwashers (U.S. or S.L. Army, "secret police,"

or whoever they may be in a given case) is *isolated* from all those to whom bonding had previously been established. The draftee is sent to boot camp and sees no loved ones (wife, girl-friend, parents, etc.) for a number of weeks or months. The political prisoner is thrown into a dungeon. Patty Hearst was locked in a closet as soon as she was "rebirthed" out of the trunk of the car. Experiments in isolation by the U.S. Marine Corps, Dr. John Lilly and others -- and the records of shipwrecked sailors, as summarized by Lilly in *Simulations of God* -- show that only a few hours of pure isolation may be necessary before hallucinations begin. These hallucinations, like those of psychedelic drugs, indicate the breaking down of previous imprints and the onset of vulnerability to new imprints.

The need to bond the bio-survival circuit to somebody (or some *thing*) is indicated by the giraffe who imprinted on the hunter's jeep as a mother-substitute. Similarly, children without siblings, especially those in remote rural areas, often invent imaginary playmates, which can become "real" enough to frighten the parents into suspecting the onset of psychosis. Dr. Lilly's records of sailors and explorers in isolation show that such "guides," "companions" or "holy guardian angels" reappear quickly even in adulthood when normal social contact is removed. They also come promptly to those undergoing the mysterious state called "near-death" or "out of body experience," (e.g. when the heart stops on the operating table.)

The first human being who appears to the subject after this isolation can easily become bonded as the mother-substitute, or, next best, as a father-substitute. This explains why people held prisoner by terrorists (e.g. on highjacked airplanes) often develop a "paradoxical" sympathy for those who are threatening to kill them. It also explains why the draftee begins to look on his kidnappers as protectors as well as captors, and why the brainwash victim begins to please, gratify and eventually "respect" the brainwasher.

In all cases, since the bio-survival circuit is keyed to nourishment, those who bring food become possible subjects for bonding. The political prisoner, the draftee, the subject kidnapped by terrorists, all move somewhat closer to identification/bonding with their captors as they are fed regularly. Again, this is imitated crudely by various religions (without the terror that creates true imprint vulnerability) by following baptism/rebirth rituals with a communal meal or Holy Eucharist.

Adaptations of these principles can be applied even to those who walk into the brainwashing environment voluntarily at first, as in People's Temple, the Manson Family, and similar organizations. The first step, once the victim is inside the territory (commune), is to begin *isolation* by cutting off all communication with the outer world and its conflicting reality-tunnels. Meanwhile, a parental-protective atmosphere is quickly created (sometimes called "love-bombing") and *food* is provided.

Whether the subject has entered voluntarily as in these communes, or has been kidnapped or arrested (as in police states), the next stage is to break down the second circuit emotional-territorial imprints. That means that the subject continues to be fed (maintaining first-circuit oral dependence) while the second circuit ego is attacked in every manner possible. A point-by-point camparison of the techniques of a Synanon "gamer" and U.S. Army drill sergeant, for instance, would show astonishing similarities, since the basic message is dozens and dozens of variations on "You are all *wrong*. We are all *right*." It is extremely unlikely that somebody as *wrong* as you will become *right*, ever, but we will try to teach you." The anal vocabulary of territorial status is, of course, employed extensively. The ideal subject may almost forget his or her name and become conditioned to answering to "You ass-hole, come here."

The sense of bottom dog helplessness can be escalated by periodic doses of real terror. One of Charlie Manson's famous sayings was "Fear is the great teacher," and every brainwasher would agree ardently. In communist countries (as dramatized in Costa-Garvas's fine and factual film, *The confession*) a favorite trick is to take the subject out of his cell, march him to a courtyard, place a noose about his neck, and convince him he is about to be hanged. The relief, when this turns out to be a bluff, creates ideal imprint vulnerability. A variation in my novel *Illuminatus* has the victim persuaded he has been poisoned, dumped in a coffin and the lid slammed upon him. Those who have been initiated as Mark Master Freemasons will recognize at once that the same technique is the "mark that you will carry to your grave."

Among the Zuni Indians, the male at adolescense is kidnapped by masked "demons" who carry him away from the tribe (away from mother and other imprinted security figures.) He is dragged out into the desert and threatened with whips. Then the masks come off, revealing his maternal uncles, and in that moment of imprint vulnerability the tribal "secrets" (the local reality-tunnel) are explained in a way that leave an indelible mark on his consciousness. Similar rites of passage are found in all tribes, few as cleverly designed as this one. Symbolic and diluted versions survive in Bar Mitzvahs and Confirmation ceremonies in our local mega-tribes.

The rebirthing of the second circuit is (relatively) complete when the Bottom Dog subject begins to seek, sincerely (not hypocritically) to win the approval of the Top Dogs. This, of course, only begins as play-acting; the skilled brainwasher knows that, and does not really object. With subtle reinforcement the play-acting becomes more and more genuine. Edmund Burke noted long ago, and every Method Actor knows, that you cannot make three dramatic gestures of rage in a political speech, without beginning to feel some real rage. You cannot make three gestures of submission without beginning to feel really submissive. (this is the psychology of the "company man," who truly *identifies* with his employer after years of obedience.)

The draftee first tries to please the sargeant, to avoid further humiliation and punishment. Gradually, he genuinely *wants* to please the sargeant, i.e. to prove he is not *all wrong* and is "good enough" to be a soldier. Patty Hearst undoubtedly pretended to accept the SLA reality-tunnel at first, and gradually found the pretence becoming more and more real.

This process is accelerated by a system of occasional rewards, as the subject more and more often *emits* (as the Behaviorists would say) the desired behaviors. Since people are more compli-cated than Behaviorists know, it is necessary to vary this with occasional punishments for "insincerity," or "backsliding," so that the subject learns that *after* the initial stage, *it is not enough to pretend to accept the new reality-tunnel*; to escape further humiliation, ego-loss, terrorism and permanent Bottom Dog status, *one must begin to accept it sincerely.* After the imprint of helplessness had been made, this conditioning and learning will proceed fairly smoothly, especially if the Chief Brainwasher's confederates reinforce it with encouragement, support, and general "reward" (for sincere submission) and contempt, disappointment and general rejection (for insincerity or backsliding.) Re-imprinting the third semantic circuit can now follow easily. The human brain is capable of mastering any symbol-system if sufficiently motivated. Some people can even play Beethoven's late piano music, although to me this is as "miraculous" as any feat alleged by psychic researchers; people can learn French, Hindustani, differential calculus, Swahili, etc. ad. infinitum -- *if motivated.* When the first circuit security needs have been re-imprinted and second circuit ego-needs have been hooked to mastering a new semantic reality-tunnel, that tunnel will be imprinted.

At this point a certain amount of arbitrary nonsense is of great value. That is, the new reality-tunnel (like the old one) or symbol-system should contain pitfalls (gross violations of previous reality tunnels and common sense) so that the subject can be accused of backsliding (being "all wrong," after all) and thereby incited to try harder to become part of the new reality-tunnel.

Thus, Jevovah's Witnesses may not accept blood transfusions, even if their life depends on it: harder still (since all mammals have an instinct to protect their young) they must reject blood transfusions for their children, even if the children die of this neglect. A Roman Catholic woman may not be divorced even if her husband comes home drunk every night, beats her up and gives her V.D. In the U.S. Marines, a recruit who commits the hideous crime of calling a rifle a "gun" must walk around the base with his rifle in one hand and his penis in the other reciting to everybody he meets, "This is my rifle/ This is my gun/ This is for fighting/ This is for fun." Theosophists were once required to believe that there is a hole at the North Pole going down to the center of the earth; Manson required his followers to believe the hole was in the Mohave Desert. Nazi Party members were asked to believe that the lion is an Aryan animal and the rabbit non-Aryan. Etc.

The neurological and sociological function of such "nonsense" (which makes the Rationalist gasp in shock) is to sharply segregate those within the new reality-tunnel from those outside. This makes for group solidarity, group-reinforcement, and a strong sense of alienation and discomfort when on rare occasions it is necessary to talk at all with those outside the brainwasher's semantic system. The group must ensure, of course, that this alienation is experienced as "superiority." Those who are outside the reality-tunnel must be perceived as "all wrong" -- just as the subject was, before being brainwashed.

Drugs can be, and have been, used to fine-tune these processes, but the general neurological principles are powerful enough that it is quite likely that many famous cases of brainwashing were accomplished as above described, without any drugs at all -- e.g. the American soldiers who confessed to war crimes which they evidently had not committed, the loyal Communists who confessed to Trotskyite conspiracies which seemingly never existed, etc. It takes very few weeks for most armies, without drugs, to convert a civilian into a soldier, even though the two species are as different as Roman Catholics and Shintoists.

In one of my Immortal Novels I describe a religious cult called Loonies, founded by one Neon Bal Loon, in which members pray in pig-Latin while standing on one leg like storks. This is considered satire, but any would-be messiah who understands the above principles could create such a cult easily; and the members would soon have a quite sincere sense of superiority to those outside that reality-tunnel.

Cults and outlaw terrorists generally follow the above procedures by further rewiring of the fourth, socio-sexual circuit. (Governments usually leave that circuit alone, since government agents are largely puritanical-authoritarian and afraid to get involved at all with raw Eros.) It is no secret that the most powerful secret society of the middle ages, the Knights Templar, forced recruits to participate in both blasphemy and sodomy. Just as the deliberate nonsense of all cultish third circuit semantics isolates the group from the rest of society, this initiation separated the Templars from the rest of Christendom; the alienation could easily be conditioned into a sense of superiority. The Mau-Maus in Kenya also insisted on one act of homosexuality to break the new member's previous conditioning toward heterosexuality and monogamy. Other cults, some quite well known, attempt to repress sexuality entirely -- another way of breaking the statistically normal imprinting of the fourth circuit.

The Manson Family insisted on what might be called, oxymoronically, compulsory free love. The Army serves normal amative bonds and casts the subject into a world where compulsory celibacy alternates with whore-house adventures and, quite often, the rape of enemy women, with homosexuality as an ever-present hidden option. A current American guru, Da Free John, imprints his subjects for lifelong monogamy, almost like the outside U.S. culture, but is indifferent as to whether these pairings are heterosexual or homosexual. Whatever variation the cult-leader may choose, what makes for successful "separate reality" is that it be in some respect outlandishly different from that of the major society.

The easiest way to get brainwashed is to be born. All of the above principles then immediately go into action, a process which social psychologists euphemistically call *socialization.* The bio-survival circuit automatically hooks onto or bonds to the most appropriate mother or mothering object; the emotional-territorial circuit looks for a "role" or ego-identification in the family or tribe; the semantic circuit learns to imitate and then use the local reality-grids (symbol systems); the socio-sexual circuit is imprinted by whatever mating experiences are initially available at puberty.

The subjects may not come out of this process ready to murder women and children, like the graduate of boot camp, or even willing to believe that Charlie Manson was both Jesus and Satan simultaneously, or willing to spout New Left slogans while robbing banks. The subjects come out of normal "socialization" *depending on where and when they were born* as Eskimo totemists, Moslem fundamentalists, Roman Catholics, Marxist-Leninists, Nazis, Methodist Republicans, Oxford-educated-agnostics, snake worshippers, Ku Kluxers, Mafiosos, Unitarians, I.R.A.-ists, P.L.O.-ists, orthodox Jews, hardshell Baptists, etc. etc. etc.

The universe or existence, is obviously large enough and complex enough and the ego self-centered enough, that all of these reality-tunnels are capable of "making sense," to some degree, to those imprinted/conditioned to accept them. It is also obvious that most of these reality-tunnels contain elements so absurd that everybody *not* imprinted/conditioned by them looks at them with astonishment and dismay, wondering "How can a rational person (or peoples) believe such rubbish?"

What the Thinker thinks, the Prover proves . . . whether you are living in a Christian reality-tunnel, a Mansonoid reality-tunnel, an Immortalist reality-tunnel, a vegetarian reality-tunnel, a Rationalist reality-tunnel . .
Everybody has the only true *true* religion.
Earlier, we quoted some words from Persinger and Lafreniere:

> **We, as a species, exist in a world in which exist a myriad of data points. Upon these matrices of points we superimpose a structure and the world makes sense to us. The pattern of the structure originates within our biological and sociological properties.**

It is to be hoped that this makes more sense to the reader now than it did at the beginning of our enquiry.

The function of the domesticated primate brain, insofar as we have described it up to this point and leaving out the higher, newer circuits, is to serve as an "organ of adaptation" in Freud's phrase. Specifically, the oldest, most primitive, most mechanical centers serve simple bio-survival. The more recent (500,000,000-year-old, roughly) emotional territorial centers serve to maintain pack identity, habitat-space and hierarchy. The distinctly hominid semantic circuit (100,000-year-old?) makes maps and models -- reality-tunnels -- which we tend to confuse with reality itself, and, worse yet, with "all" of reality. The (30,000? year old) moral-social circuit creates the domesticated adult personality, or parent-role, or super-ego.

Now, obviously the third, semantic circuit works *with* and *for* these other antique circuits. The maps and models it makes are tools of adaptation, and what they adapt us to is social roles in domesticated primate society. Thus, a Midwestern Methodist is not "misusing his brain" as Arthur Koestler thinks in constructing a Midwestern Methodist tunnel-reality; that is precisely what his brain is for, to adapt him to the Midwestern Methodist tribal system -- to impose the structure of Midwestern Methodist ideology upon the myriad of data-points he encounters in his life-time. The Chinese Maoist, the Iranian Moslem, the New York Feminist, the Marin County Hedonist, etc. each has a similar, equally arbitrary, equally complex reality-tunnel. Each tunnel is also *equally absurd* when seen from outside.

The problems of the modern world arise from the fact that these reality-tunnels are no longer isolated from each other. Throughout most of human history and up to 100 years ago -- up to 20 years ago, in some parts of the world -- a man or woman could lead their entire life snugly within the cocoon of the local tunnel-reality. Today, we all constantly collide with persons living in wildly different tunnel-realities. This creates a great deal of hostility in the more ignorant, vast amounts of metaphysical and ethical confusion in the more sophisticated, and growing disorientation for all -- a situation known as our "crisis of values."

The average person has a deluge of contradictory and conflicting reality-tunnels impinging on him or her, with little training in either cultural or neurological relativism. *Speed of travel has increased by a factor of 1000 since 1900, and speed of communication by a factor of 10,000,000,* according to J.R. Platt. The deluge is accelerating and intensifying. One symptom is the fact that *TV Guide* has been taken over by a band of terrified conservatives, who cannot understand and can only dread this downpour of "alien" signals; instead of being merely a guide to what is on the tube, *TV Guide* has become a continuous wail that the tube's tunnel-reality is wider, stranger and more varied than the narrow tunnel-vision of the small-town WASP.

"WHADDYA MEAN...
TUNNEL VISION!!"

There has also arisen a *profession* of "deprogrammers," so-called. These are neuro-technicians who will, for a fee, kidnap a child (even a "child" over 21) who has wandered off, departed the parental reality-tunnel and been brainwashed into the competing reality-tunnel of some *new* (i.e. *not established -- not acceptable yet*) "cult." This is known as restoring the victim to normalcy.

It is all hypocrisy and neurological ignorance, of course. The "de-programmers" are actually *re-programmers*. The parental tunnel-reality is as arbitrary (and, to an outsider, as bizarre) as that of any "cult." A special system of tricky semantics allows most people and some courts to ignore these facts. Just imagine what would happen if a wayward child of Methodist parents had wandered into the Roman Catholic Church, say, and the parents attempted to have that child coercively "de-programmed" (re-programmed) into Methodism; or if the child had joined the U.S. Army, like Calley, and the parents kidnapped him and tried to re-program him into civilian reality-tunnels.

These problems will not go away; and the abrasions they cause, as various brainwashed robots continue to collide with each other, will accelerate. Speed of travel and of communication are still continuing to accelerate.

Fortunately, higher circuits are forming in the human brain and offer broader vistas than the narrow tunnel-visions of the antique circuits. That is the topic of our concluding chapters.

Since everybody "prefers" one circuit over the others, there are people in each society who are easily recognizable as Narcissists (first circuit robots), Emotionalists (second circuit robots), Rationalists (third circuit robots) and Moralists (fourth circuit robots).

Rationalist robots, like the other robots, may be totally mechanized or may have some slight flexibility, or "freedom" built into their circuitry. The totally robotized make up the vast horde of the Fundamentalist wing of the Materialist church and the other True Believers in the scientific paradigms of 1968, 1958, 1948 or whenever their nervous systems stopped taking new imprints.

These are the people who are perpetually frightened and dismayed by the large portion of human behavior mediated through Circuit II mammalian politics. They think that because this territorial-emotional ("patriotic") behavior is not Rational, it should not exist. They accept Darwin as dogma, but are nervous about "Darwinism" (because it accepts mammalian politics as an Evolutionary Strategy that has worked thus far) and are repulsed by the data of ethology, genetics and sociobiology. They don't like the rest of the human race much, because it is not guided by their favorite circuit, and they are uneasily aware that the rest of the human race does not like *them* much.

These Rationalist robots are also very uncomfortable with the newer circuits -- and some of them spend most of their lives writing articles and books devoted to "proving" that the newer circuits do not exist and that all scientists who have recorded the behavior of these newer circuits are liars, fools, bunglers, charlatans or some manner of Damned Heretics.

Like the Emotional robot, the Moralistic robot, the Narcissist robot etc., the Rationalist robot cannot be "argued" out of his narrow reality tunnel. We can only emphasize, one more time, that each and every reality-tunnel created by a domesticated primate brain is a finite cross-section of that brain's personal history; and each such finite reality-tunnel is as "personalized" as the music of Bach or Beethoven, the paintings of Rembrandt or Picasso, the novels of Joyce or Raymond Chandler, the comedy of the 3 Stooges or Monty Python, the religions of Roman Catholicism or Zen Buddhism, the politics of Libertarianism or the I.R.A., the architecture of St. Peter's or Disneyland . . .

And each of these art-works seems like "reality" to the people who have created them and live in them. Rationalism is just another such group art-work, a little less tolerant than most, a little more useful to technologists than any other, a little stupid when it can no longer transcend the last paradigm it has created.

The totally robotized Rationalist, the one whose nervous system has stopped growing entirely, can be recognized by two signs:

He or she is constantly trying to prove that much of the daily experience of the rest of humanity is "delusion," "hallucination," "group hallucination," "mass hallucination," "mere coincidence," "sheer coincidence," or "sloppy research."

And he or she never thinks that any of his or her own experience would fit into any of those categories.

EXERCIZES

1. Become a pious Roman Catholic. Explain in three pages why the Church is still infallible and holy despite Popes like Alexander VI (the Borgia Pope), Pious XII (ally of Hitler) etc.

2. For those of you who remember Mai Lai, become Lt. Calley. Say aloud, and really *feel and believe,* "The Army comes first. I'm for the Army all the way." If you don't remember try Jerry Falwell. Say aloud, and really *feel and believe,* "Help us fight moral decay, send your checks in today."

3. Refute this whole book. Demonstrate that everybody else has been brainwashed but you and your mother (father) has the one, real, *objective* view of the universe.

4. Accept this book, if not in whole at least in general outlines. Assume you have been brainwashed. Try to learn as much from every human you meet about their separate reality-tunnel and see how much of it you can use to make your reality-tunnel bigger and more inclusive. In other words, *learn to listen.*

5. James Joyce said he never met a boring human being. Try to explain this. Try to get into the Joycean head space, where everybody is a separate reality-island full of mystery and surprise. In other words, *learn to observe.*

6. Read Aldous Huxley's *The Genius and the Goddess.* Note how the Circuit III scientific Genius reverts to Circuit I helpless infant when his wife leaves him.

7. After experimenting with the Nazi reality-tunnel, the Catholic reality-tunnel etc., re-enter your "normal" reality-tunnel. Does it still seem totally objective, or do you begin to recognize how much of it is your own software and hardware running programs?

8. Finally, explore the tunnel-busting reality of Chistopher S. Hyatt's book titled *Undoing Yourself With Energized Meditation and Other Devices.* What tunnel-reality is he selling and how sincere is he about his writing? Also do you think he has read my work and I his, or is this last statement a gimmick of the publishers played on two innocent authors and the trusting public or even worse did I write his book, or could it be, that we are one and the same?

CHAPTER ELEVEN

THE HOLISTIC NEUROSOMATIC CIRCUIT

But there is also in us an aspiration for the mastery of Nature . . . Health, strength, duration, happiness and ease, liberation from suffering, are part of the physical transformation which . . . evolution is called upon to realize.

Sri Aurobindo,
The Future Evolution of Man

THE RESURRECTION OF THE BODY NEED NOT BE POSTPONED UNTIL AFTER DEATH. IT CAN HAPPEN AT ANY MOMENT.

This is a copy of Crowley's inspired drawing, for his original see the book of Thoth or study his Tarot deck.

The beast with four heads represents the antique circuits; the hedonic "laid-back" nude is neurosomatic rapture. The serpent is "the rising of the kundalini serpent," a Hindu metaphor for imprinting this Circuit V neurosomatic bliss-control.

> Calling all downs. Calling all downs to dayne. Array! Surrection!....It is just, it is just about to, it is just about to rolywholyover.
>
> James Joyce, Finnegans Wake

The word "psychosomatic" has been around long enough to be generally understood; unfortunately, it is another semantic spook. The concept of "psyche" or "soul" was borrowed from the theologians, who, being bankrupt, are in no position to lend anything. What we know and experience -- our tunnel-reality -- is what registers on the brain and nervous system.

The phenomena of "faith healing," "regeneration," "rejuvenation," bliss, ecstasy, rapture, etc. have been occurring for many thousands of years, in all known cultures. In the pre-scientific language of yesterday's psychology we would refer to such events as "psychosomatic." In our deliberately modernistic and almost sci-fi jargon, we prefer to call them *neurosomatic*.

The neurosomatic circuit of the brain is much more recent than the antique circuits previously discussed. It does not manifest in all human beings, and appears late in life, usually, to those who do activate and imprint it.

Temporary neurosomatic consciousness can be acquired by (a) the yoga practice of *pranayama* breathing and (b) for those who can handle it, by ingestion of Cannabis drugs, such as hashish and marijuana, which trigger neurotransmitters that activate this circuit.

Of the former device, *pranayama*, Aleister Crowley -- certainly the most skeptical of all mystics -- writes forcefully:

> For mind and body alike there is no purgative like pranayama, no purgative like pranayama.
> For mind and body alike, for mind and body alike -- alike!
> --there is, there is, there is no purgative like pranayama -- pranayama! -- pranayama! yea, for mind and body alike there is no purgative, no purgative, no purgative (for mind and body alike) no purgative like pranayama!

If this is not emphatic enough, Crowley adds elsewhere:

> Pranayama is notably useful in quieting the emotions and appetites . . .Digestive troubles in particular are very easy to remove in this way. It purifies both the body and the mind and should be practised certainly never less than one hour daily by the serious student.

To which he adds a footnote:

Emphatically. Emphatically. Emphatically. It is impossible to combine pranayama properly performed with emotional thought (second circuit reflexes -- R.A.W.). It should be resorted to immediately, at all times during life, when calm is threatened.

This is very strong stuff from the mystic who filled his books with jokes and jeers, and who always told his students, not "Believe me," but "Don't believe me." About pranayama, for once in his life, Crowley was serious.

In the experience of this author, pranayama will remove all forms of depression, including profound grief and bereavement; it will sooth anger and remove resentments; it seems beneficial to all minor health problems and -- occasionally -- major health problems. Hindus, who are professionals at pranayama, claim a great deal more, such as: immunity to pain of all sorts, *Samadhi* ("union with God"), levitation, etc.

Most notably, pranayama creates neurosomatic Turn on: *sensory* enrichment, *sensual* bliss, *perceptual* delight, and a general laid-back Hedonic "high." Similar effects are produced by *voluntary* isolation in a Lilly tank, by zero-gravity (the astronaut's "mystical" experiences are all of this neurosomatic variety) and, for the judicious or lucky, Cannabis drugs, as said above.

Negative neurosomatic circuit effects are experienced by amateur yogis, by many pot-heads, and by a large number of schizophrenics. The neurosomatic feedback loop, in these unfortunate cases, reverses the above description. *Sensory* experience becomes unpleasant (any sound or touch is painful), *sensuality* turns into acute discomfort with the entire body, *perceptions* warp into nightmare, and general anxiety is imprinted. Light is particularly terrifying and painful, often associated with Hell or with "death-ray machines" manipulated by unscrupulous enemies.

Gopi Krishna, a Hindu bureaucrat who took up yoga originally only for health reasons, was abruptly catapulted into a negative neurosomatic state for several years. *All* sensations were so painful that he many times thought he would die. The details, in his autobiography, *Kundalini,* are pathetic, and sound much like schizophrenia. He came out of this finally, entered a positive neurosomatic state, and has been writing blissful books about the Perfection of the All, typical of this circuit, ever since.

Nikola Tesla, the Yugoslav genius, went through the same "Hell" or schizoid state, without yoga, in his teens. He came out of the horrors with the scientific theory of alternating currents worked out, a belief in extra-sensory perception, a superhuman memory, and a streak of visionary humanitarianism that led him into continuous conflicts with the corporations that financed his more-than-100 major electrical inventions. (He earned over $1,000,000 before the age of 30, at a time when $1,000,000 was a lot of money, and he died broke, trying to sell an invention he said would abolish poverty.)

Most shamans, and many mystics, have been through similar negative-to-positive neurosomatic sensitization. Christian Scientists call it *"chemicalization."* St. John of the Cross called it, poetically, the Dark Night of the Soul. Cabalists call it "crossing the Abyss."

In Kazanazkis's *The Odyssey: A Modern Sequel,* Odysseus sees a statue which seems to him urgently meaningful. The statue was Kazanzakis's symbol for the evolution of these circuits, which have been known (more or less) in various symbolisms for a few thousand years. E.g. the "seven souls" of the Egyptians, the ten "lights" of the Cabalists, etc.

The Kazanzakis statue shows an animal (Circuit I), a warrior above the animal (Circuit II), a scholar above the warrior (Circuit III), a lover (Circuit IV), a face in agony ("chemicalization" the "Dark Night of the Soul", the "crossing of the Abyss" which equals the entry to Circuit V the hard way), a face in bliss (successful Circuit V re-imprinting) and a man turning into pure spirit (Circuit VII). Circuit VI is missing in the schemata, as Circuit IV is missing in Jung, and everything above Circuit III is missing in Carl Sagan.

Some lucky souls jump to Circuit V bliss without passing through the horrors of "chemicalization" and the "Dark Night of the Soul."

The neurosomatic circuit is "polymorphous perverse," in Freud's unappetizing terminology. This merely means that the nervous system itself, taking over as driver, is now directing the rest of the body. "Every act (becomes) an orgasm," said Aleister Crowley, giving his own Tantric emphasis to the polymorphous nature of this circuit.

The lives of the saints are full of stories which seem "miracles" to the four-circuited majority, or are rejected as "lies, hoaxes, yarns" by the three-circuited dogmatic Rationalist, but which seem perfectly normal from the viewpoint of five-circuited polymorphous consciousness. The saint says he is in rapture, and full of gratitude to God, for giving him such a feast for dinner as -- plain *bread* and *water*. (Of course, many a pot-head will understand *that* degree of neurosomatic rapture . . .) The guru comes into the room and his bio-energy* has such a charge that a cripple jumps up and is "healed"; the cripple merely acquired neurosomatic turn-on *by contact*, as some people get "contact high" when others are on drugs. The fire-walkers in many shamanic traditions walk on the fire, as they tell enquiring anthropologists, to prove their control over "the spirit" -- i.e. to *demonstrate* to themselves and others that they have achieved high-quality neurosomatic tuning.

One faith-healer told the present author, "Most people die of adrenalin poisoning." In our terminology, most people have too much first-circuit anxiety and second-circuit territorial pugnacity for their own good. They are literally *struggling for survival*, as no other animals do, despite Darwin. Most animals simply *play* most of the time, solve problems of survival when they have to, or die of not solving the problems; only humans are *conscious of struggling,* and hence worried and depressed about the Game of Life.

The faith-healer went on, "What cures them is realizing that *I'm* not afraid." That is, contact with a fifth-circuit personality, a person who controls his or her own Circuit II adrenalin-trips, can be a catalyst, throwing the sufferer upward into a personal fifth-circuit experience.

The *avant-garde* 20% of the population, due to the Consciousness Movement (a secularization of much ancient shamanic wisdom), already understands every "wild" idea in the last few pages. They have had enough neurosomatic experience to know that they were once totally robotized (as most people still are) and are knowingly engaged in acquiring more neurosomatic know-how. *When this reaches 51% of the population, a major historical revolution will have occurred, as profound as the Life Extension*

---

*By which we mean nothing "mystical." It is now known that many *physical* energies radiate from the body, and that even *chemical* effects can be transmitted (experienced as emotional "vibes") from one person to another, the chemicals acting as stimuli to trigger neurotransmitter actions in the second person.

Revolution.*

In McLuhan's terms, the fifth circuit is "non-linear" and "global." That is, it is not limited by the one-thing-at-a-time sequences of the semantic circuit; it *thinks in Gestalts.* This is why it is so often connected with "intuition," which is a way of thinking between and around data-points on the perceptual screen -- sensing what total field the points must be part of.

The great musician has developed a remarkable feedback between fifth circuit *Gestalt*-ing and the third circuit function of coding such "coherent structures" into the inspired symbolism of music. Music always leads to some right-brain activity in listeners, and the fifth circuit is almost certainly located in the right brain hemisphere.

Beethoven, we remember, was left-handed. Since the *left hand* is neurologically linked to the polymorphous *right brain*, one might say he was genetically inclined to right brain activities, that is, to sensing coherent *wholes*, to plunging into neurosomatic bliss almost "at will," and to sensory-sensual raptness and rapture. Everybody "knows" that the Sixth Symphony is "pantheistic," but whether Beethoven was an ideological pantheist or not, that way of responding to nature is normal and natural right-brain Circuit V functioning. That is, anybody on the Fifth Circuit will *"talk like a pantheist"* whether or not he has developed a "philosophy" about pantheism. The miracle of Beethoven is not that he felt the universe that way -- a few thousand fifth circuit types throughout history have also felt and sensed nature that way -- but that he mastered the third circuit art of music with such skill that he could *communicate such experiences,* which is precisely what the ordinary "mystic" cannot do.

The neurosomatic circuit probably began to appear around 30,000 years ago. (That is the conclusion of Barbara Honnegger, who has made a profound study of European cave paintings, coming to the conclusion that many of them show *exercizes to increase right-brain activity* similar to those still used in surviving shamanic and yogic traditions.)

This fifth circuit is bonded into the *right cortex* and neurologically

*Please re-read this sentence, and think about it.

linked to the *limbic* (first circuit) *system* and the *genitalia*. These neural links explain the sexual metaphor of "kundalini" or "serpent" energy used to describe this circuit in systems as varied as Indian Tantra, Gnosticism and Voodoo, and the Chinese *yin-yang* (male-female) energies associated with it.

Prolonged sexual play without orgasm always triggers some Circuit V consciousness.

It is quite easy to determine if the Fifth Circuit has been activated successfully or not. How often does a person go to a doctor? If a mind researcher is "glowing" rather than greyish, "bouncy" rather than draggy, if he or she has a "sparkle" -- and if he or she virtually *never* goes to a doctor -- the neurosomatic circuit has been mastered. As Mary Baker Eddy once wrote (thereby making herself hugely unpopular with those who love to talk of matters mystical but have no empirical knowledge):

> "The Word was made flesh." Divine Truth must be known
> by its effects on the body as well as on the mind.

There is no tribe known to anthropology which doesn't have at least one neurosomatic technician (shaman). Large-scale outbursts of neurosomatic consciousness have occurred frequently in all the major historical periods, usually being stamped out quickly by the local branch of the Inquisition or the A.M.A.; other outbursts have been co-opted and diluted.

As we read in the New Testament:

> And when he had called into him his twelve disciples, he
> gave them power against unclean spirits, to cast them out,
> and to heal all manner of sickness and all manner of disease ..
> And as ye go, preach, saying, the kingdom of heaven is at
> hand. Heal the sick, cleanse the lepers, raise the dead, cast
> out devils: freely ye have received, freely give.
> (Matt 10: 1-8)

It may or may not have happened exactly like that; as Mark Twain would say, there might be a few stretchers in there. But something like this, however much the evangelist may exaggerate it, must have happened to account for Christianity's rapid triumph over other, but probably less effective, systems of opening the fifth circuit. Mithraism, the Eleusinian cult at Athens, the

Dionysiac cults, etc. all had age-old shamanic techniques for inducing neurosomatic rapture; Christianity *(at first)* seems to have been superior in creating neurosomatic *control.* In St. Paul's metaphor, the "Old Adam" (Circuits I-IV) got bleached out, and the "New Adam" (Circuit V) took over as the center of consciousness and self-government. In another metaphor, the body became the flexible clay and the awakened (illuminated) brain became the sculptor.

In general, fourth circuit problems take the form of *guilt*; "I cannot do what I am supposed to do." Third circuit problems take the form of *perplexity*; "I cannot understand how I got into this mess, or how to get out of it, or what is expected of me," etc. Second circuit problems take the form of *bullying* or *cowardice*: "I will force them, or I will surrender and let them force me." First circuit problems take the form of *body symptoms*: "I feel rotten all over" gradually centering in, under enough stress, on one acute disabling symptom.*

Fifth Circuit neurosomatic consciousness bleaches out all these problems at once. The disappearance of first-circuit "physical" illnesses only *seems* more "miraculous" than the transcendence of second-circuit emotionalism, third-circuit perplexity and fourth-circuit guilt. It is the Cartesian mind/body dualism that makes us think of such first-circuit "physical" cures as somehow stranger or more spooky than any rapid improvement on the other circuits.

One of the intents of our terminology is precisely to transcend that Cartesian dualism, making all the circuits equally comprehensible within one context.

The robotized Rationalist fears and resents Circuit V rapture and its holistic intuitive faculties (just as the robotized Emotionalist fears and resents Circuit III reason). Thus, when the neurosomatic circuit feedback begins to function, and the mutated Circuit 5 person tries to describe his or her rapture and at-oneness, the Rationalist hastily mutters that this is "merely subjective."

Misery is "merely subjective," too, but that doesn't keep it from hurting. The neurosomatic skill of transmuting all experience, so that one is high and happy in a situation where the four-circuited majority would be miserable, is worth learning for the very

*This last is Eric Berne's "Wooden Leg" game, which asks to be relieved of social participation or interaction on the grounds of being physically *hors de combat.*

simple, egotistic reason that it's more fun to be happy than to be in agony. It is also socially beneficial, because, as some 1960s sage remarked, "You can't *do* good until you *feel* good." Just as misery loves company, the high and happy want everybody else to be high and happy. (This first lesson the fifth circuit adept has to learn is to control this upsurge of altruism and not make a nuisance of oneself by trying to *force* everybody to be happy . . .)

The Rationalist is even more alarmed by the results of prolonged fifth-circuit bliss, which includes the ability to heal a wide variety of diseases both in oneself and in others. Even the well-documented current research on endorphins -- which gives us the beginning of a neuro-chemical explanation of how such healings operate -- is regarded with dis-comfort or hostility by the more robotized Rationalists. It all sounds "metaphysical" and therefore it cannot exist.*

There is nothing supernatural about the fifth circuit. It merely appears "supernatural" by comparison to the earlier circuits; but the third circuit, of which the Rationalist is so proud, undoubtedly appeared "supernatural" when it first appeared. (The Egyptians attributed speech and writing, third circuit functions, to divine intervention by the god Thoth.) The fifth circuit, like the earlier circuits, is just another evolutionary mutation, necessary to us as we move toward a more complex neuro-social level.

"It's just like ordinary life, except that you're always a foot above the ground," says an old Zen proverb.

This "floating" aspect of the fifth circuit is preparing us for extraterrestrial migration.

One of the most interesting neurosomatic adepts in all history, from the viewpoint of the present theory, was Mary Baker Eddy. Precisely because Mrs. Eddy was fundamentally naive and unaware of most of philosophy, she never realized that you cannot speak or write about the Ineffable. She therefore wrote about it at length. If her writings are hard to decipher, if they often sould like "the ravings of a disordered mind" (Aleister Crowley's description of mystic writings, including his own), they also have moments of astonishing lucidity. For instance, she knew and wrote with total clarity that illness is fear and love is its

*Endorphins are neurotransmitters that trigger Circuit V. They can be activated by cannabis drugs, psychedelics, meditation, pranayama, or *visualization of white light*. The last is the most common system used by "faith-healers" and was known to the medieval Rosicrucians.

cure. Most psychologists are just beginning to comprehend that today, over 100 years later.

"Perfect love casteth out fear" and that is how neurosomatic awakening cures disease.

As Mrs. Eddy told one enquirer, "Love, love, love! That's all you have to know to be a healer." 60 years later, unheeded by most of his profession, a Scottish psychiatrist, Ian Suttie, wrote that "The physician's love heals the patient."

Another quote from Mrs. Eddy is appropriate at this point:

> When understanding changes we shall gain the reality of life, the control of soul over sense...This must be the climax, before harmonious and immortal man is obtained and his capabilities revealed.

To the ordinary scientifically-educated reader, this is metaphysical gibberish. Let us try to re-translate it into our own neurological metaphors:

> When the brain develops its full potentials we shall gain a new view of life and the control of neurosomatic bliss over lower-circuit guilts, perplexities, emotions and "body symptoms" . . .This is evolutionarily scheduled to occur before sixth circuit evolutionary awareness and physical immortality are achieved.

We suggest that Mrs. Eddy, having activated a large part of the right brain hemisphere, was able to think in Gestalts as well as serving as transmitter of neurosomatic "healing" to others. She was looking down the DNA highway to the scientific breakthroughs of the decade in which we now live.

Many have turned on the neurosomatic circuit due to prolonged illness, especially if they grow impatient with doctors and resort to self medication and/or faith-healing. The bathroom of Nietzsche, according to Stefan Zweig, looked "like a pharmacy shop," due to the large number of drugs and medicines with which the philosopher treated his chronic migraines. Gurdjieff employed cocaine, hashish and yoga techniques (probably including pranayama) to treat the incessant and increasing pains resultant from his war wounds and two car accidents. The "harshness" of these two philosophers, their contempt for ordinary human suffering, their visions of the superhuman state beyond emotion and pain, all probably derived from neurosomatic Turn Ons alternating with acute pain. That is, they experienced the whole of evolution from the lower circuits to the full development of neurosomatic bliss, and were expressing chiefly contempt for their own relapses into less-than-blissful consciousness.

In the East, the control of the neurosomatic circuit is known as *dhyana, cha'an* or *Zen;* the state is sometimes called "Buddha-mind" or "Buddha-body." To the ancient Greeks, where rituals to achieve it with psychedelic drugs were performed yearly at Eleusis, those who accomplished the ritual successfully were called *digenes*, "twice-born." The metaphor lingers in the "born again" terminology of charismatic Christianity, and is symbolized by the myth of the Resurrection of the Body.

Freud recognized this state, vaguely, as the "oceanic experience." Gurdjieff calls this circuit the Magnetic Center.

Faith-healers and adepts of a few yogic schools seem to live in neurosomatic consciousness permanently; most who have achieved it at all tend to have it only in flashes, as noted by Ezra Pound:

> Le Paradis n'est pas artificial
>   but is jagged
> For a flash,
>   for an hour.
> Then agony,
>   then an hour.

This *"Paradis,"* this condition of neurosomatic ("mind-body") peace, should be considered a new brain circuit toward which all humanity is evolving, slowly and painfully, out of mammalian antique circuits. This progression, from primate emotion to post-hominid tranquility, from "man" to "super man." is the Next Step that mystics forever talk of; you can hear it in most of Beethoven's later, major compositions.

As mentioned before, governmental brainwashers are generally too puritanical to handle, or manhandle, the socio-sexual circuit and content themselves with mind-washing and brain-programming on the bio-survival, emotional and semantic circuits, while outlaw bands like the S.L.A. or Mansonoids go further and re-imprint the socio-sexual circuit also.

It is necessary to note that some cults presently active on this backward planet go even further than that and engage in *neurosomatic brainwashing*.

A *permanent* neursomatic circuit can only be imprinted by prolonged practise of one of the yogic, Tantric or related sciences, and perhaps good genes, good environments and good luck generally.

Neurosomatic brainwashing -- the most powerful form of robotization -- consists in *temporary* activation of the neurosomatic circuit by the brainwasher, together with assurances that *only* the brainwasher (or the "god" who "acts through him") can turn on this circuit.

For full effect, this is, of course, preceeded by normal brainwashing, The victim is first isolated from his or her previous environment and trained to hook the bio-survival circuit onto the "guru" and/or the Ashram or commune. The emotional circuit is bent and broken by continuous attacks upon status (ego), until the only emotional security left is found in Total Submission to the group reality-island. The re-infantilized victim is then ready to imprint any semantic circuitry desired, from EST to Krishna to People's Temple, etc. The socio-sexual circuit can then easily be programmed for celibacy, for free love, or for whatever sexual game the guru has selected. *Then, and only then, the neurosomatic buttons are pushed and ecstasy is "given" to the subject "by" the guru.*

Marjoe Gortner, a long-time practitioner of this science, commented ironically in a film made after abandoning it for a different careeer, "The marks never realized they could do it" (push the neurosomatic buttons) "for themselves. They all think they need me jacking them off!" Gortner is, nowadays, unusually honest. The average charismatic *insists* that the victims can never learn to do it for themselves.

One of the greatest historical practitioners of this neuroscience was Hassan i Sabbah, who used relatively simple techniques, including, evidently, a time-release capsule invented by the *Sufi* College of Wisdom in Cairo.

As I describe Hassan's technique -- based on historical records -- in my novel, *The Trick Top Hat:* Two young candidates dine with Hassan; the food is laced with a time-release capsule. When asleep the candidates are taken to Hassan's famous "Garden of Delights." The capsule had released a heavy does of opium and they were quite thoroughly unconscious and unaware of their surroundings.

The garden -- officially known as the "the Garden of Delights" -- covered several acres. Here candidates were prepared for admission to the Order of the Assassins: they were to become the most feared and legendary professional killers in history. But here also, in this same garden, were prepared candidates for admission to the Brotherhood of Light, the Illuminati. The candidates, in fact, were prepared the same way. They themselves selected, unknown to themselves, which order they would enter --the political Assassins or the mystic Illuminati.

Both young men were conveyed into the Garden of Delights and placed several acres apart from each other. In a short time, the second stage of the time-release capsule began to work; cocaine was released into their bloodstreams, thereby overwhelming the traces of the soporific opium and causing them to awaken full of energy and zest. At the same time, as they woke, hashish also began to be released, so they saw everything with exceptional clarity and all colors were jewel-like, brilliant, divinely beautiful.

A group of extremely comely and busty young ladies -- imported from the most expensive brothel in Cairo -- sat in a circle around each of the young candidates, playing flutes and other delicately sweet musical instruments. "Welcome to heaven," they sang as the awakening men gazed about them in wonder. "By the magic of the holy Lord Hassan, you have entered Paradise while still alive." And they fed them "paradise apples" (oranges), far sweeter and stranger than the earth-apples they had known before, and they showed them the animals of paradise (imported from as far away as Japan, in some cases), creatures far more remarkable than those ordinarily seen in Afghanistan.

"This *is* heaven!" the first young man exclaimed, in ecstasy. "Great is Allah, and great is the wise Lord Hassan Sabbah!"

But, twenty acres away, surrounded by similar lovely ladies and other wonders, the second young man mercly gazed about him, smiled in contentment, and said nothing.

And then, in both cases, the *houris* of Paradise, as promised in the *Koran*, began to dance, and as they danced, they discarded one by one each of their seven veils. As the veils were thrown off, more and more hashish was released from the capsules and the young men saw with greater clarity, felt with deeper intensity, experienced beauty and sexual joy in a way completely unknown in their previous earth lives.

Then, as each young man sat entranced by the beauty and wonder of Heaven, the *houris* finished the dance, and nude and splendid as they were, rushed forward in a bunch, like flowers cast before the wind. And some fell at the candidate's feet and kissed his ankles; some kissed knees or thighs, one sucked raptly at his penis, others kissed the chest and arms and belly, a few kissed eyes and mouth and ears. And as he was smothered in this hashish-intensified avalanche of love, the lady working on his penis sucked and sucked and he climaxed in her mouth as softly and slowly and blissfully as a single snowflake falling.

In a little while, there was no more hashish being released and more opium began to flow into the bloodstream, the young candidates slept again; and in their torpor, they were removed from the Garden of Delights and returned to the banquet hall of the Lord Hassan.

There they awoke.

"Truly," the first exclaimed, "I have seen the glories of Heaven, as foretold in *Al Koran*. I have no more doubts. I will trust Hassan i Sabbah and love him and serve him."

"You are accepted for the Order of Assassin," said Hassan solemnly. "Go at once to the Green Room to meet your superior in the order."

When this candidate had left, Hassan turned to the second, asking, "And you?"

"I have discovered the First Matter, the Medicine of Metals, the Elixir of Life, the Stone of the Philosophers, True Wisdom and Perfect Happiness," said he, quoting the alchemical formula. "And it is inside my own head!"

Hassan i Sabbah grinned broadly. "Welcome to the Order of the Illuminati!" he said, laughing.

Hassan i Sabbah was not the first or last student of the ways in which sexuality can be transmuted into fifth circuit rapture. Further to the East, there were Tantric schools within Hinduism, Buddhism and Taoism, which taught techniques by which prolongation of the genital embrace could explode into dramatic brainchange. In the West, underground cults of Gnostics, Illuminati, alchemists and witches kept similar techniques as closely-guarded secrets, for if the Holy Inquisition ever learned of such practices the participants would be denounced as devil-worshippers and burned at the stake.

In our own time, there has been a revolutionary upsurge of these ancient neurological secrets, with an admixture of more modern techniques. Tantric teachers are available in many cities. Masters and Johnson use quasi-Tantric practices to treat sexual dysfunctions. As early as 1968, a poll by McGlothlin showed that 85% of the pot-smokers in the country said their chief interest in the Weed was its function as enhancer of erotic sensation. Vibrators and other sexual toys proliferate; Gays come out of the closet; philosophers of a culture without repression (Norman Brown, Henri Marcuse, Charles Reich) become best-sellers.

Saul Kent, a writer on medical science for general audiences, has even suggested that electronic sexual surrogates can and will be manufactured in the near future. (Your own Marilyn Monroe doll!) Instead of joining Tom Wolfe and the neopuritans in throwing up our hands in horror at such an idea, let us consider it for a moment. Let us see if we can peek outside our imprinted-conditioned reality-tunnel.

If a sexual android is possible in 1995 or 2005 or whenever, why not a totally programmed sexual environment? Let us call this, in memory of Herman Hesse, the Magic theatre. We start with what is concurrently available in high-priced brothels in the hedonic Sun Belt section of America.

Massage, a first-circuit tranquilizer, has all the advantages of the opiates without being habit-forming. Our Magic Theatre, then, would include computerized body-relaxers-and-energizers better than current massage techniques.

Porn movies are available, for stimulation, in the better brothels. Our Magic Theatre would have them in 3D on all four walls, obviously.

Marijuana and stimulants like cocaine or speed are available in brothels everywhere. Our Magic Theatre would have better chemical rapture-agents.

One can go on adding details, according to personal fantasy, until one has created a room in which bliss can be extended in all dimensions, indefinitely.

A strange thing has happened in constructing this cyberneticized brothel. We seem to have gone beyond sex to something that might be called meta-sex. While specific genital pleasure might still be fun, it is hardly as important as it seemed to us before we came into the multi-dimensional Pleasure Dome where all senses are stimulated to ecstasy.

And the most peculiar thing about this bawdy science-fiction projection is that we don't even need to build a Magic Room. It is built into our brains already. We have been describing the positive neurosomatic consciousness which Freud called "polymorphous perversity" in one of his Puritan moods and "the oceanic experience" in one of his mystical moments. This is what the neurosomatically turned-on brain feels like.

In alchemy this was known as "the multiplication of the first matter" or "the Philosopher's Gold," which was unlike ordinary gold in that it could not be *spent* or used-up, since it perpetually multiplied and renewed itself. It is the "Third Eye" of the Illuminati tradition, which transforms all it sees; the eye of which Jesus speaks in his gnomic aphorism, "The light of the body is the eye; if therefore thine eye be single, thy whole body will be full of light." (Matt 6:22)

EXERCIZES

1. Get the lesson book from the local Christian Science Reading Room and read the lessons for a month.

2. Attend a Sufi week-end seminar.

3. Acquire my *Sex and Drugs* and try the Tantric exercizes there described.

4. Learn how to do pranayama properly, from an expert. (I have tried describing this elsewhere, and have found there is no way to prevent gross errors in verbal transmission of this nonverbal knowledge. Get a Hindu to *show* you.)

5. Da Free John, an American guru, says you can reach Illumination by constantly asking, "Who is the One who is living me now?" Well -- is it Circuit I consciousness, Circuit II ego, Circuit III mind, Circuit IV sex-role, Circuit V Gestalt-field, or a higher circuit?

Who is it? Where is it? *How old* is it?

6. Dr. Aiden Kelly has suggested that the so-called "unconscious" is *more conscious* than the so-called conscious mind. That is, the "unconscious" contains all the feedbacks of the neurosomatic circuit and the other circuits that maintain life. Consider this idea. Is this the "One who is living you now"?

CHAPTER TWELVE

THE COLLECTIVE NEUROGENETIC CIRCUIT

It is no longer only the Right that is conservative. The entire Left is also suddenly conservative. The liberal and the radical Left have fallen behind.

F.M. Esfandiary, Upwingers

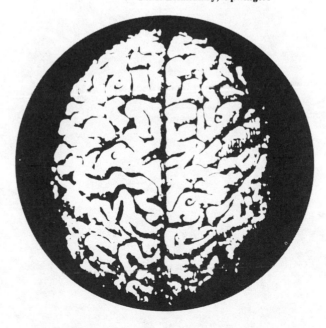

The sixth circuit of the brain kicks into action when the nervous system begins to receive signals from *within the individual neuron* -- from the RNA-DNA "dialogue," the neurogenetic feedback system.

The entire nervous system, including the brain, has been designed like the rest of the body, by the "code" within the DNA molecule, which sends signals via messenger RNA molecules to tell the organism what to do: *Grow red hair. Have blue eyes. Stand up and walk now. Start to talk. Find a mate.* Etc. Our entire mental lives -- our brain hardware and software -- exist within the perimeters of this DNA master-tape.

With neurogenetic consciousness, these DNA archives become accessible to brain scanning, *while awake.* (They are always accessible, as archetypes of the Jungian "collective unconscious," during dreaming sleep.)

The first to achieve neurogenetic awareness, a few thousand years ago, spoke of "memories of past lives," "re-incarnation," "immortality," etc. That these neurological adepts were speaking of something real, in the best language of their day, is indicated by the fact that many of them (especially Hindus and Sufis) gave marvelously accurate poetic vistas of evolution milleniums before Darwin and foresaw Superhumanity before Nietzsche.

The Greeks called this "the vision of Pan," the Chinese "the great Tao," Hindus "Atman consciousness." The numinous, aweful, sublime "God" "Goddess" and "Demon" figures who appear in the initial stages of this Awakening are Jung's "archetypes of the collective unconscious" and are recognized as "vistors from dream-time" by primitives, as "them from Sidde" by witches, as the Weird People in a thousand folk-traditions.

Gurdjieff calls this circuit the True Emotional Center.

The "akashic records" of Theosophy, the "phylogenetic unconscious" of Dr. Stanislaus Grof, the "Gaia hypothesis" of biologists Margulis and Lovelock -- which holds that the biosphere of this planet is one intelligent organism -- are three modern metaphors for this circuit. The visions of past and future evolution described by those who have had trans-time experiences during close-to-death or "clinical death" trauma also describe the Circuit VI neurogenetic reality-tunnel.

Specific exercizes to trigger neurogenetic imprints are not to be found in yogic teaching; it usually happens, if at all, after many years of expertise in the kind of advanced rajah yoga that develops Circuit V somatic bliss. Heavy does of LSD, of course, always trigger temporary neurogenetic vistas.

The neurogenetic circuit is best considered, in terms of current science, as the genetic archives activated by excitement of anti-histone proteins -- the DNA memory coiling back to the dawn of life and containing also the genetic blueprints for the future of evolution.

"I am He that was, and is, and shall be," a sentence from the Egyptian *Book of the Dead*, in hieroglyph and in his own hand-writing, was found on the desk where Beethoven composed the Ninth Symphony and all his later, aeon-spanning "evolutionary" music. One judges from this, and from the music itself, that Beethoven had opened the neurogenetic circuit.

Here dwell primordial archetypes, far older than language yet newer than tomorrow, Personifying this circuit as a being, Crowley tells us:

> . . .the "Babe in the Egg of Blue" (cf. the final image of Kubrick's *2001* -- R.A.W.). . .represents the Higher Self. . .The connection is with the symbolism of the dwarf in mythology. . .In his absolute innocence and ignorance he is "the Fool"; he is the Savior. . .the "Great Fool" of Celtic legend, the "Pure Fool" of Act I of *Parsifal*. . .he is also the Green Man of spring festivals. . .So we see him fully armed as Bacchus Diphues, male and female in one, the bisexual Baphoment, and. . .Zeus Arrhenothelus, equally bisexual. . .(He is shown in this full form in the Tarot Trump XV, "The Devil"). . .But the "small person" of Hindu mysticism, the dwarf insane yet crafty of many legends in many lands, is also this same. . .Silent Self of a man, or his Holy Guardian Angel.

These images are not poetic whimsies by Crowley. They reap-pear in the dreams of individuals (the personal myth of the night), in the myths of all peoples (the impersonal dreams of the species), and, of course, over and over in UFO contact stories.

STUDY THE NEXT TWO IMAGES CAREFULLY

Circuit 6 neurogenetic consciousness: This symbolizes a pan-like god, displaying the concept of genetic memories symbolized by the human-animal seed-forms in the testicles.

Another archetype from the neurogenetic archives ("collective unconscious"). The Great Mother symbolizing the genetic memories as illustrated by the flower, bird, etc.

The "language" of this circuit is the multi-level language of *Finnegans Wake,* where Finnegan is Finn-again, Finn Mac Cool of Irish legend reborn and Huck Finn again also, sailing down "Missus Liffey, " both the river Anna Liffey in Ireland and Huck Finn's Mississippi; where Mark the Wan is King Mark, cuckolded by Tristan, but Mark the Twy is Mark Twain, married to a wife he called "Livvy" just like the Irish river, and Mark the Tris is cuckolded Mark and cuckolding Tristan in one; while Marcus Lyons is all of them, plus Mark the apostle, his emblematic lion (always shown with him in medieval art), Leo the lion, Leo in the zodiac and all associated fire-signs, and one of the Four Old Men (Matt Gregory, Marcus Lyons, Luke Tarpey and Johnny McDougall) who haunt the dreamer all night long, symbolizing the four evangelists, the four bedposts surrounding the sleeper, the four antique circuits, the four suits of Tarot or ordinary playing cards, the four elements of the ancients, and all the other fours that Jung has found omnipresent in the "collective unconscious." To parallel the evolution of the first four circuits in human (and mammalian) history, Joyce also offers the four stages of the development of the "Gracehoper" (egg, larvae, chrysalis, adult) and such dream-logical quartifications as "eggburst, eggblend, eggburial, and hatch-as-hatch can," "their weatherings and their marryings and the buryings and their natural selections," "a human (pest!) cycling (pist!) and recycling (past!) and there he goes (pust!) again," etc.

This archetypal circuit is replete with what Jung called *synchronicities -- meaningful coincidences -- which he attributed to the circuit's roots in what he called the "psychoid" level, below the personal and* collective unconscious, where "mind" and "matter" are not yet differentiated -- the royal highway of the DNA-RNA-CNS (central nervous system) telegraph, in our metaphor.

Such synchronicities are a sure sign that you are dealing with the neurogenetic circuit. For instance, in a *Finnegans Wake* study group, we were all convulsed with laughter when noticing that "Toot and Come Inn" is not just a parody of American cutesy-pie motel names but another of Joyce's countless puns on Tutankhamen. At this point, my wife entered the room to enquire what was so funny. When we explained, she said, "That's a synchronicity -- I was just watching a T.V. program about Tutankhamen." And, of course, Joyce put the boy-king into the

the dream because the main theme of *Finnegans Wake*, the main theme of the neurogenetic circuit, is the survival of genetic memory through time, symbolized by the Resurrection myth; and Tut was dug up (resurrected) synchronistically, just after Joyce started work in this epic.

As Joyce explains the logic of the neurogenetic circuit, "This ourth of years is naught save brickdust and being humus the same roturns"(the earth gives back, in new forms, what is buried) since "on the bunk of our breadwinning lies the cropse of our seed-father" (comment superfluous, to those who know *The Golden Bough*) and "Phall if you but, will rise you must." The seed, the genetic code, and the egg, cellular wisdom, sends the signal down the aeons; in the similar metaphor of Nobel geneticist Hebert Muller, "We are all giant robots manufactured by DNA to make more DNA."

To the individual, the breaks in the chain of life/death/life/death-life/death are all-too real and painful; to the seed-and-egg wisdom of the neurogenetic circuit, the seamless unity of lifedeathlife-deathlife-deathlife is the greater reality.

The neurogenetic circuit is probably located in the *right neocortex* and is more recent than the neurosomatic circuit in the back sections of the right cortex.

Circuit V neurosomatic consciousness allows you to "converse" with the evolutionary architect who *designed* your body --and billions and billions of others since the dawn of life around 3-4 million years ago.

This "architect" is the greatest designer on this planet, as Bucky Fuller has often commented. No human architect has yet equalled Her efficiency *or* Her esthetics in such routine products as roses, eggs, insect colonies, fish etc.

She (or He) can be personified in modern terms as Mother DNA or Father Nucleic Acid. The Rationalist immediately objects that such personification, however inescapable it is to all who have encountered the Architect directly on this circuit, is illegitimate, because She or He is *unconscious*. The rebuttal, given by all Circuit VI adepts in all cultures and all ages, is that She or He is not unconscious but intoxicated, and it is a divine intoxication.

Less poetically, whether we "humanize" this "architect" into a

Big Momma or Big Daddy, or *"animalize"* it into a jackal-headed being like the Egyptian, or *"insectualize"* it into a divine Preying Mantis like one African tribe, or *"spiritualize"* it into something totally abstract like Hindus and Christian Scientists, we are only depicting one cross-section of this 3-4 billion-year-old Being. When we *"moleculize"* it as DNA we are also only seeing one cross-section -- *the most useful cross-section for scientific analysis.* That is all that needs to be said, or should be said, for the "scientific materialist" chemicalization of the biosphere, and it is no contradiction of *direct experience* of the Being itself via Circuit VI yogas, biological or chemical. Indeed, the direct experience undoubtedly can and has helped many scientists get a wider, more holistic view of what is going on in evolution, which they have brought down to Circuit III in better linguistic models. Teilhard de Chardin is one, but not the only, example of a scientist whose evolutionary model has been improved by such direct Circuit VI experience.

For those who have not yet had Circuit VI experience -- and most of humanity will possess the technology to turn on this circuit at will, within the next twenty years -- this evolutionary perspective might, possibly, be conveyed by a series of quantum jumps in perspective, thus:

The individual can make mistakes, even fatal ones. Consciousness of Circuits I-V is far from infallible; we all get into messes, and sometimes they kill us.

The gene-pool can make mistakes, but less frequently. Most gene-pools have a life-span far beyond any individual, by a factor of many thousands. Obviously, if we judge intelligence by survival, gene-pools -- made up of the information of many million individuals -- are more "intelligent" than any individuals, even geniuses. (Einstein was not as smart as the Jewish people collectively. He created Relativity and was smart enough to escape the Nazis. The Jews, historically, created dozens of ideas as important as Relativity and survived hundreds of pogroms.)

The species is even more intelligent than the gene-pool. It lives millions of times longer than any individual, many thousand times longer than any gene-pool.

The biosphere -- Gaia -- the DNA script -- is more intelligent than all individuals, gene-pools and species. It has survived *everything* thrown at it for nearly 4 billion years, and is getting smarter all the time. It is on the edge of achieving immortality; through the sixth circuit it has a better eye to see itself and judge its trajectories than ever before; it is getting ready to leave this planet and expand across the universe.

Beethoven, to cite him one more time, said "Anybody who understands my music will never be unhappy again." That is because his music is the song of the Sixth Circuit, of Gaia, the Life Spirit, becoming conscious of Herself, of Her powers, of Her own capacities for infinite progress.

EXERCIZES

1. List *at least* 15 similarities between New York (or any large city) and an insect colony, such as a bee-hive or termite hill. (If you can't think of at least 15, read Edward Wilson's *Sociobiology.*) Contemplate the *information* in the DNA loop, which created both of these enclaves of high coherence and organization, in primate and insect societies.

2. Read the *Upanishads* and everytime you see the word "Atman" or "World Soul," translate it as DNA blueprint. See if it makes sense to you that way.

3. Contemplating these issues usually triggers Jungian synchronicities. See how long after reading this chapter you encounter an amazing coincidence -- e.g. seeing DNA on a license plate, having a copy of the *Upanishads* given to you unexpectedly, seeing an image like Crowley's Pan or Great Mother in a work of popular art etc.

4. Explain such a synchronicity, when it occurs, in Circuit III Rationalist terms -- mere coincidence etc.

5. Psychologist Barbara Honnegger explains synchronicities by saying that the right brain hemisphere (where this circuit is located) moves you in space-time to the place where the synchronicity will occur, while the Rationalist left brain invents rationalizations to go there. Synchronicities are a language through which this circuit communicates with the left brain, in this theory. Try explaining coincidences by that theory. What messages is your right brain trying to send to your left brain?

6. Jung and several of his disciples (e.g. Coleman, Steiger, Fideler) have suggested that UFOs are messages from this collective DNA circuit to the left brain. What do such messages mean? What is the right brain trying to tell us?

CHAPTER THIRTEEN

THE RELATIVITY
FACTOR

It is the human situation that is basically tragic. Right and
Left revolutionaries cannot alter this basic dilemma. For
instance, the most radical Left-wing group has no program
to overcome death. The entire Right-Left establishment is
still death oriented.

F.M. Esfandiary, Upwingers

CAN 100,000 PEOPLE HALLUCINATE AT ONCE?
How else do you explain history?

I once saw a cartoon -- I forget where -- that seems to me to summarize the central fact of neurological relativism.

A cat approaches a dog and says "Meow." The dog looks confused. The cat repeats, "Meow!" The dog still looks confused. The cat repeats, more emphatically, "MEEOW!!!" Finally, the dog ventures, "Bow-wow?" The cat stalks away indignantly, thinking "Dumb dog!"

Of course, human communication, and our great philosophical debates, cannot be on this primitive level. *Of course!*

Nonetheless. . .

Between May and October, 1917, in Fatima, Spain, occurred the best documented series of "miracles" in modern history. As everybody knows, it began when three illiterate peasant girls had a vision of the Blessed Virgin Mary. Please note at once that it is easy, and tempting, for the Rationalist, and the non-Catholic generally, to treat this first incident as "merely" hallucination. *Note next how hard it is to make that explanation stick* as the subsequent details are narrated.

At the second "visitation of the Virgin" in June there were *fifty witnesses.* All agreed that they heard an explosion and saw a puff of smoke. (Only the three girls on this and subsequent occasions ever saw the Lady.) Shall we assume now that, in addition to hallucinating girls we must add *a practical joker with a smoke-bomb,* to make sense of what was going on?

At the third visitation in July there were *4500 witnesses.* All of them heard an explosion again, at the Lady's departure, and most of them claimed they heard humming and buzzing noises while the children spoke to her. (This humming and buzzing is common in later UFO stories. . .)

On August 13, there were *18,000 witnesses,* who saw, or hallucinated a symphony of weirdities, including flowers falling out of the sky, another explosion, bright flashes of light on the clouds and on the ground (crimson, pink, yellow and blue) and a luminous globe spinning through the sky, just like a modern UFO.

On September 13, there were *30,000 witnesses.* All saw the luminous "UFO" again, and there was another downpour -- not flowers this time, but glistening globules of light that got smaller as they descended and "melted" near ground level. Dr. Carl Sagan will solemnly tell you, with his bare face hanging out, that all 30,000 witnesses were hallucinating simutaneously.

October 13, the last "miracle" was witnessed by *70,000 at the scene,* and *30,000 others* for hundreds of miles around claimed to see some of the phenomena. Some said that the sun plunged directly toward the earth, but others that a globe "big and bright as the sun" had appeared and did the plunging. This was accompanied by flashes of red, violet, blue and yellow, together with a "heavenly" perfume permeating the air.

It is claimed that "thousands" of people were converted to Catholicism by these events. Please note that if it had all happened 50 years later in 1967, many of these people would have been converted to the newer mystique of the Space Brothers.

Nietzsche once said, "We are all greater artists than we realize." It is a function of the above record (and this book as a whole) to make that obscure joke totally clear to every reader.

But, but, but -- All 100,000 witnesses who saw some of the phenomena associated with the last Fatima "miracle" must have been hallucinating, of course. This is the most comfortable and conservative way of dealing with such events, and one does not have to be as narrow as Dr. Sagan to prefer such a simple explanation. Still. . .if 100,000 people can hallucinate simultaneously, and if, as history assures us, many millions can share a "religious" or political delusion simultaneously, only a man as rigidly dogmatic as Sagan can avoid asking the most disturbing questions about the origin of his own beliefs and perceptions.

Cromwell once addressed the Irish rebels, saying, "I beseech you, in the bowels of Christ, think it possible that you might be wrong." History does not record that Cromwell ever addressed the same remark to himself.

Each of us is trapped in the reality-tunnel (assumption-consumption) his or her brain has manufactured. We do not "see' it or "sense" it as *a model our brain has created.* We automatically, unconsciously, mechanically "see" and "sense" it *out there,* apart form us, and we consider it "objective." When we meet somebody whose separate tunnel-reality is obviously far different from ours, we are a bit frightened and always disoriented. We tend to think they are mad, or that they are crooks trying to con us in some way, or that they are hoaxters playing a joke.

Yet it is neurologically obvious that no two brains have the same genetically-programmed hard wiring, the same imprints, the same conditioning, the same learning experiences. We are all living in separate realities. That is why communication fails so often, and misunderstandings and resentments are so common. I say "meow" and you say "Bow-wow," and each of us is convinced the other is a bit dumb.

According to reliable statistics, over 100,000,000 citizens of the U.S. "believe in" UFOs and *at least* 15,000,000 have seen a UFO. The system of ideas, rumors, myths, hopes etc. clustered about the UFO phenomenon may be *the most powerful sociological force* for change currently acting upon our society, as Dr. Jacques Vallee recently stressed in an address to a special United Nations committee on the UFO mystery.

The UFO debate, or quarrel, hinges upon the two categories which we find central to our thesis -- the innocent-looking ideas of "inside" and "outside." Broadly speaking, the UFO "skeptics" are those who claim the UFO is "inside" the UFO observor ("hallucination," mis-identification, etc.), while the UFO "believers" claim the UFO is "outside" (objectivity).

As the semanticist Alfred Korzybski often warned, when we split verbally that which is never split existentially we introduce fallacies into our thinking. Korzybski's favorite example was the matter of "space" and "time"; for in experience, we never encounter "space" without "time" or "time" without "space," i.e. a year measures the *space* the Earth moves around the sun, and the space the Earth travels in one orbit gives us the *time* we call a "year." The verbal separation of "space" and "time" became such a problem in late 19th Century physics that paradoxes and contradictions multiplied endlessly; and this was only resolved when the genius of Einstein went back before the verbal categories, realized we had created them, and started physics over from the ground up on the simple existential fact that we never encounter "space" or "time" separately but only the undifferentiated "space-time continuum."

Applying this Einsteinian operational orientation to the UFO problem, we observe that we never hear of a UFO without a human observer. In fact, even the UFOs "seen" on radar become UFOs (unidentified, rather than indentified, flying objects) through *processes of evaluation* in the *nervous system* of the radar operator.

It is, therefore, the Einsteinian and operational approach to accept the seamless unity of UFO-observer and cease to separate them into "UFO" and "observer."

The types of "critters" who appear in human-UFO experiences include the following:

Black men, blue men, green men, black-faced men with green bodies;

fish-scaled men, hairy dwarfs, huge-headed bald dwarfs, armless humanoids;

dwarfs with three fingers. dwarfs with eight fingers, claw-handed men, one-eyed men;

elephant-eared men, long-haired sexless WoMen, man-apes, man-birds;

robots, beer-can shaped entities walking on fins, headless things, dwarfs in Nazi uniforms.

This is only a partial zoology of the UFO experience.

The craft favored by this odd crew includes big blobs of light, little blobs of light, clusters of lights, hard metallic ships, flat-bottom discs, conic discs, coin-like discs, domed discs, ovals, spheres, spheroids, cigar-shaped craft, cubes, tetrahedrons, crescents, "eggs," teardrop shapes, boomerangs. This is also a partial list.

"We are being invaded by beings from dozens of galaxies," said Otto Binder, a believer in the extraterrestrial theory of UFOs, when this list was shown to him.

One consistency does appear in this confusing picture: those who have had Close Encounters show marked personality change afterwards. At one extreme we find paranoid and schizophrenic breakdowns or acute anxieties requiring hospitalization; at the other, "illuminations" similar to those of Buddha, Mohammed, Jesus, St. Paul. In the middle we find a great deal of messianic fanaticism typical of vulgar religiosity everywhere.

Other statistical clusterings can be found in the literature. *Blinding lights* are very common -- do we recall St. Paul and the thousands at Fatima? And *drumming and humming noises* are also common -- as in shamanism everywhere, at Fatima, and even in so sophisticated a brain-change system as Tibetan Buddhism.

Let nobody underestimate this phenomenon just because it is irrational. It is equally irrational for 900 people to drink cyanide because a paranoid on pep-pills tells them to, and Naziism and the Holy Inquisition were equally irrational. As Dr. Jacques Vallee told the UN committee on UFOs,

> **It is the *third aspect* of the UFO phenomenon which deserves full attention. . .The third aspect is the social belief system which has been generated by. . .the expectation of space vistors. This belief. . .*is creating new religious, cultural and political concepts* of which social science has taken little notice. (Italics in original.)***

Rationalism -- a philosophy for which we have great sympathy, as for a backward relative -- wants to take UFO "observers" by the collar, shake them vigorously and shout in their ears, "Look you so and so. It never happened! -- you got it buddy?" Well, maybe it didn't -- and then again maybe it did. In either case, UFO-observers are all better artists than they realize.

It should also be obvious that the Rationalist is a better artist than *he* realizes. Amid millions of people who have or create such experiences every day in every city on the planet, the Rationalist has created a separate reality in which such things never happen -- to him.

Flying saucers and ESP (not to mention headless Things running across the road) may seem far removed from Patty Hearst's "decision" to become a bank-robber. We are trying to show that there is an intimate connection between all the weirdities of consciousness.

The process by which we construct a kitchen chair out of a whirl of atomic energy is just as *creative* (artistic) as the processes by which Patty Hearst turned her father from a beloved parent into a Pig Imperialist.

Your whole world has been constructed that way. You are "reconciled" to death because you have been told, all your life, that everybody must die. Only the Immortalist minority -- which can be found wherever scientists, science-fiction fans, Futurists

---

*Dr. Carl Jung has compared the UFOs in general and Close Encounters in particular with the "signs and wonders" that accompanied the breakdown of Roman paganism and the rise of Christianity. It is ironic to remember that the Rationalists of that time -- the Stoics, Epicureans and other heirs of the Greek philosophical-skeptical tradition -- regarded Christianity with as much contempt as the modern Rationalist has for UFOs. They simply refused to look at what was happening, until their society was overcome by the paradigm shift to the new reality-tunnel.

and space enthusiasts gather -- is living in the separate reality that claims we no longer have to accept this axiom of despair.

The revolutionaries of any decade will become the reactionaries of the next decade, if they do not change their nervous system, *because the world around them is changing.* He or she who stands still in a moving, racing, accelerating age, moves backwards relatively speaking. Thus, there are hundreds of "Thanatological" seminars available in the once revolutionary but now-reactionary Consciousness Movement. These seminars are designed to reconcile people to death, and are about as reactionary as seminars c. 1860 designed to reconcile Black people to slavery.

Only one offshot of the Consciousness Movement, the Theta Seminars of Leonard Orr, are designed to prepare people for our oncoming immortality.

EXERCIZES

1. Buy a copy of *Christian Science Sentinel* and read all the faith healings reported that month. Note that each "miracle" is attributed to the correct teaching as transmitted by Jesus Christ and Mary Baker Eddy.

2. Buy a copy of *The Peyote Cult* by anthropologist Weston LeBarre which attributes the same effects to auto-suggestion.

3. Read *Brain/Mind Bulletin* for any recent year, and observe that similar healings are reported regularly and attributed to *endorphins* in the brain.

4. Witnesses have testified that Jim Jones (like a few other professional faith-healers) used *shills* part of the time, a shill being a person who pretends to be ill and pretends to be cured, in order to get the audience in the right frame of mind. Re-read *all* the miracles in the New Testament, using each of these filters: Jesus had the correct teaching; Jesus was using auto-suggestion; the sufferers' brains unleashed *endorphins* when Jesus gave them positive auto-suggestion; Jesus was a con-man using shills.

Since you weren't there at the time, does your choice among these theories, or your combination of them, tell more about Jesus or more about your own favorite reality-tunnel?

5. Did you ever really give a good trial to our exercize, "I can now exceed all of my previous hopes and ambitions"? *Try it*; and at the same time, try "I can be healthier than I have ever been before."

CHAPTER FOURTEEN

THE META-PROGRAMMING CIRCUIT

Man is ignorant of the nature of his own being and powers, Even his idea of his limitations is based on experience of the past. There is therefore no reason to assign theoretical limits to what he may be, or what he may do.

Aleister Crowley, Magick

According to Alfred Korzybski, any "idea" or mental state is a brain circuit which the brain itself can contemplate, thereby having an idea about the idea, or a mental state about the mental state, etc. There is no theorectical or real limit to the higher-ordering process; it is the "Infinity Within" of which mystics speak.

Dr. John Lilly says, "In the province of the mind what is believed true is true or becomes true within limits to be learned by experience and experiment. These limits are further beliefs to be transcended. In the province of the mind there are no limits."

Mind and its contents are functionally identical: My wife only exists, *for me,* in my mind. Not being a solipsist, I recognize the converse: I only exist, *for her,* in her mind. Lest the reader exclaim, like Byron of Wordworth, "I wish he would explain his explanation!", let us try it this way: If I am so fortunate as to be listening to the *Hammerklavier* sonata, the only correct answer, if you ask me suddenly, "Who are you?" would be to hum the *Hammerklavier.* For, with music of that quality, one is hypnotized into rapt attention: there is no division between "me" and "my experience."

In heavy meditation, when I think of me, I am me; when I think of me and you, I am me and you; when I think of you alone, I am not there anymore; when I think of God, I am God. *What I see with my eyes closed and with my eyes open is the same stuff: brain circuitry.*

Mathematician J.W. Dunne puts the matter in a parable. A painter, who had escaped from the asylum to which he was (justly or unjustly) confined, decided to paint the field in which he found himself. Finished, he looked at the result and realized that something was missing: namely, himself and his canvas, which were part of the field. So he started over and painted himself and his canvas in the field. But, examining the results with philosophical analysis, he realized that something was still missing: namely, himself and his canvas on which he was painting himself and his canvas in the field. So he started a third time...and a fourth...*ad infinitum.*

We think of the paintings of M.C. Escher at this point: Or we recall the old folk-tale of the farmer who set out to market with ten donkeys, on one of which he rode. After a while, he began to wonder if any of the donkeys had strayed and he began counting there seemed to be only nine. Disturbed, he dismounted and walked around the herd, counting carefully -- and there were ten after all. So he remounted and went on riding, until worry beset him again. So he counted another time. . .and there were nine. So, once again, he dismounted and walked about counting carefully, to find ten. The process is repeated until he finally solves the problem, carrying one donkey on his back and driving the other nine before him.

The "disappearing donkey" trick is the epitome of ideas about ideas about ideas, paintings of paintings of paintings, etc. The disappearing donkey is a synecdoche of the metaprogramming circuit of the nervous system.

The metaprogramming circuit -- known as the "soul" in Gnosticism, the "no-mind" *(wu-hsin)* in China, the White Light of the Void in Tibetan Buddhism, *Shiva-darshana* in Hinduism, the True Intellectual Center in Gurdjieff -- simply represents the brain becoming aware of itself. The artist seeing himself in his painting, seeing himself seeing himself in his painting . . . In the Zen metaphor, it is a mirror that reflects anything, but does not hold onto anything. It is a conscious mirror that knows it can always reflect something else by changing its angle of reflection.

This is analyzed mathematically in G. Spencer Brown's *Laws of Form;* an analog, using not Brown's math but Gödel's, and employing illustrations from the music of Bach and the paintings of Escher, is Hofstadter's *Gödel, Escher, Bach.*

Most of the occult literature of the world -- aside from the 95% of it that is sheer rubbish -- consists of *tricks, gimmicks* and *games* (which the Hindus call *upaya,* "clever ways") to trigger metaprogramming consciousness. This generally means leading the student "all around Robin Hood's barn" as many times as are necessary, until the poor victim discovers that he has created the barn himself.

For instance, a popular game with California occultists -- I do not know its inventor -- involves a Magic Room, much like the Pleasure Dome discussed earlier except that *this* Magic Room contains an Omniscient Computer.

To play this game, you simply "astrally project" into the Magic Room. Do not ask what "astral projection" means, and do not assume it is metaphysical (and therefore either impossible, if you are a materialist, or very difficult, if you are a mystic). Just assume this is a *gedankenexperiment*, a "mind game." Project yourself, in imagination, into this Magic Room and visualize vividly the Omniscient Computer, using the details you need to make such a super-information-processor real to your fantasy.

You do not need any knowledge of programming to handle this astral computer. It exists in the 1990s or early in the next century; you are getting to use it by a species of time-travel, if that metaphor is amusing and helpful to you. It is so built that it responds immediately to human brain-waves, "reading" them and decoding their meaning. (Crude prototypes of such computers already exist.) So, when you are in this magic room, you can ask this Computer anything, just by thinking of what you want to know. It will read your thought, and project into your brain, by a laser ray, the correct answer.

There is one slight problem. The computer is very sensitive to *all* brain-waves. If you have any doubts, it registers them as negative commands, meaning "Do not answer my question." So, the way to use it is to start simply, with "easy" questions. Ask it to dig out of the archives the name of your second-grade teacher. (Almost everybody remembers the name of their first grade teacher -- imprint vulnerability again -- but that of the second grade teacher tends to get lost.)

When the computer has dug out the name of your second-grade teacher, try it on a harder question, but not one that is *too hard*. It is very easy to sabotage this machine, but you don't want to sabotage it during these experiments. You want to see how *well* it can be made to perform.

It is wise to ask only one question at a time, since it requires *concentration* to keep this magic computer real on the field of your perception. Do not exhaust your capacities for imagination and visualization on your first trial runs.

After a few trivial experiments of the second-grade-teacher variety, you can try more interesting programs. Take a person toward whom you have negative feelings, such as anger, disappointment, feeling-of-betrayal, jealousy or whatever interferes with the smooth, tranquil operation of your own bio-computer. Ask the Magic Computer to *explain* that other person to you; to translate you into their reality-tunnel long enough for you to understand how events seem to them. Especially, ask *how* you seem to them.

The Poet Prayed:

Oh would some power the giftie gie us
To see ourselves as ithers see us

This computer will do that job for you; but be prepared for some shocks which might be disagreeable at first.

This super-brain can also perform exegesis on ideas that seem obscure, paradoxical or enigmatic to us. For instance, early experiments with this computer can very profitably turn on asking it to explain some of the propositions in this book which may seem inexplicable or perversely wrong-headed to you, such as "We are all greater artists than we realize" or "What the Thinker thinks, the Prover proves" or "mind and its contents are functionally identical."

This computer is much more powerful and scientifically advanced than the rapture-machine in the neurosomatic circuit. It has total access to all the earlier, primitive circuits, and over-rules any of them. That is, if you put a metaprogramming instruction into this computer; it will relay it downward to the old circuits and cancel contradictory programs left over from the past. For instance, try feeding it on such metaprogramming instructions as:

1. **I am at cause over my body.**
2. **I am at cause over my imagination.**
3. **I am at cause over my future.**
4. **My mind abounds with beauty and power.**
5. **I like people, and people like me.**

Remember that this computer is only a few decades ahead of present technology, so it cannot "understand" your commands if you harbor any doubts about them. Doubts tell it not to perform. Work always from what you can believe in, extending the area of belief only as results encourage you to try for more dramatic transformations of your past reality-tunnels.

This represents *cybernetic consciousness;* the programmer becoming self-programmer, self-metaprogrammer, meta-meta-programmer, etc. Just as the emotional compulsions of the second circuit seem primitive, mechanical and, ultimately, silly to the neurosomatic consciousnes, so, too, the reality maps of the third circuit become comic, relativistic, game-like to the meta-programmer.

"*Whatever you say it is, it isn't,*" Korzybski, the semanticist, repeated endlessly in his seminars, trying to make clear that third-circuit semantic maps are not the territories they represent; that we can always make maps of our maps, revisions of our revisions, meta-selves of our selves.

"*Neti, neti*" (not that, not that), Hindu teachers traditionally say when asked what "God" is or what "Reality" is.

Yogis, mathematicians and musicians seem more inclined to develop meta-programming consciousness than most of humanity. Korzybski even claimed that the use of mathematical scripts is an aid to developing this circuit, for as soon as you think of your mind as mind[1] and the mind which contemplates that mind as mind[2] and the mind which contemplates mind[2] contemplating mind[1] as mind[3], you are well on your way to metaprogramming awareness. *Alice in Wonderland* is a masterful guide to the metaprogramming circuit (written by one of the founders of mathematical logic) and Aleister Crowley soberly urged its study upon all students of yoga.

R. Buckminster Fuller illustrates the metaprogramming circuit, in his lectures, by pointing out that we feel puny in comparison to the size of the universe, but only our bodies (hardware) are puny. Our minds, he says -- by which he means our software --*contain* the universe, by the act of comprehending it.

The seventh, metaprogramming circuit is the most recent in evolutionary time and seems to be located in the *frontal lobes*. That is why the traditional Hindu exercize to activate it is to fix the consciousness in the front of the forehead and hold it there, hour after hour, day after day, year after year, until the metapro-grammer awakes and you begin to perceive-create infinite realities where before there was only one static jail-cell "reality" in which you were trapped.

As said above, this circuit is the "soul" of the Gnostics, as distinct from the self. The self seems to be fixed and firm, but is not; that is, whatever circuit you are operating on at the moment is your "self" at that moment. If I point a gun at you, you go to

Circuit I consciousness at once, and that is your "self" at that instant. But if you are sexually attracted to somebody, you go to Circuit IV and that is your "self" until you are orgasmically satisfied (or hopelessly frustrated). Most of the preliminary exercizes in Sufi and Gurdjieff schools consist in making you aware that the "self" is not constant but shifts back and forth between the imprints on the various circuits.

The "soul" or Circuit VII is constant, because it is, as the Chinese say, void or no-form. It plays all the roles you play -- oral dependent, emotional tyrant, cool rationalist, romantic seducer, neurosomatic healer, neurogenetic Evolutionary Visionary -- but it is none of them. *It is plastic.* It is no-form, because it is all forms. It is the "creative Void" of the Taoists.

If this begins to sound like nonsense, that is inevitable on this level. As Lewis Morgan notes, in books on linguistics there always comes a point at which the prose itself becomes wildly incomprehensible, disintegrating into nonsense.

The same happens, Morgan notes, beyond a certain point in modern mathematics:

> **Gödel's Theorem was once explained to me by a patient, a gentle mathematician, and just as I was taking it all in, nodding appreciatively at the beauty of the whole idea. . .it all turned into nonsense inside my head.**

It happens in both linguistics and mathematics, because it *happens in consciousness itself* and language and math are just models of consciousness.

"Mind" is a tool invented by the universe to see itself; but it can never see all of itself, for much the same reason that you can't see your own back (without mirrors). Or as Alan Watts liked to say, because the tongue ultimately cannot taste the tongue.

Ideas about ideas -- mathematics about mathematics (Gödel) language about language -- consciousness of consciousness the whole seventh circuit brings us into what Hofstadter calls *Strange Loops.* Like the legendary ko-ko bird, we follow our own tail around in ever-narrowing circles, but unlike that mythic bird we never complete the process by flying up our own rectums and disappearing. It just seems like we're about to self-destruct in that colorful way, and we decide that what we have been reading, or thinking, or perceiving, must be "nonsense."

It is not nonsense. We are merely confronting infinity where we least expected to encounter it -- in our own lonely selves.

Physics joined linguistics, mathematics and psychology in this meta programming hall of mirrors when Schrödinger demonstrated that quantum events are not "objective" in the Newtonian sense. For fifty years since then, physicists have been struggling to build a system that will get them out of this Strange Loop. The results have been as funny as a Zen *koan*.

For instance, Niels Bohr proposed the Copenhagen Interpretation, which merely says, in the manner Gödel, that our equations do not describe the universe really. They describe the mental processes we have to put ourselves through to describe the universe. True enough -- and this whole book is a Copenhagen Interpretation of psychology and owes *everything* to Dr. Bohr but we are still in a Strange Loop, and most physicists want to get out.

Dr. John von Neumann proved that there was no way out. This is technically known as Von Neumann's Catastrophe of the Infinite Regress, and it merely shows that any device that will get us out of the first Strange Loop (the Copenhagen collapse of objectivity) will just lead us into a second Strange Loop; and any way out of that will lead to an inexorable third Strange Loop; and so on, forever.

Everybody is still trying to refute von Neumann; but nobody has been successful.

"I can't get out -- my horns won't fit through the door. . ."

The metaprogramming circuit is *not* a trap. As Joyce would say, it only looks as like it as damn it. Simply accept that the universe is so structured that it can see itself, and that this self-reflexive arc is built into our frontal lobes, so that consciousness contains an infinite regress, and all we can do is make models of ourselves making models. . .

Well, at that point, the only thing to do is relax and enjoy the show.

This is what the Hindus call *Shivadarshana,* or the divine dance. You are still in life, or life is in you, but since there are infinite aspects to everything, especially to the "you" who is observing/creating all these muddles and models, *there are no limits.*

The only sensible goal, then, is to try to build a reality-tunnel for next week that is bigger, funnier, sexier, more optimistic and generally less boring than any previous reality-tunnel.

And once you have built that bigger, funnier, happier universe of thought, build a bigger and better one, for next month.

EXERCIZES

1. If all you can know is your own brain programs operating, the whole universe you experience is inside your head. Try to hold onto that model for at least an hour. Note how often you relapse into feeling the universe as *outside* you.

2. Consider the belief system or reality-tunnel of an educated reader 1200 years ago -- in 783 A.D. How much of that tunnel still seems "Real"? How much in our reality-tunnel was unknown or invisible then?

3. Consider the reality-tunnel of an educated person 1200 years from now -- in 3183 A.D. How much of our reality-tunnel will still seem "Real"? How much of the 3183 A.D. reality-tunnel is unknown or invisible to us?

4. Re-read Moses' encounter with I AM WHO I AM in Deuteronomy. Try the theory that Moses was talking to his own metaprogramming circuit.

CHAPTER FIFTEEN

DIFFERENT MODELS AND DIFFERENT MUDDLES

It* is not just a riot of blots and blurs and
disjointed jottings linked by spurts of speed...
it only looks as like it as damn it.

James Joyce, Finnegans Wake

*Presumably the input (software) or the brain (hardware). Or both.

"REALITY" IS THE TEMPORARY RESULTANT OF CONTINUOUS STRUGGLES BETWEEN RIVAL GANGS OF PROGRAMMERS.

And every moment is a new and shocking
Transvaluation of all we have ever been.
                                T.S. Eliot, Four Quartets

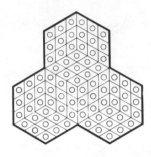

When a paradigm shift occurs -- when we go from seeing things one way to seeing them another way -- *the whole world is remade.* All that we "know" is what registers on our brains, so what you perceive (your individual reality-tunnel) is made up of nothing but thoughts -- as Sir Humphrey Davy noted when self-experimenting with nitrous oxide in 1819, and as Buddha noticed by sitting alone until all his social imprints atrophied and dropped away.

The Copernican Revolution in astronomy, the Darwinian revolution in biology, the Relativity and Quantum revolutions in physics, have all been as shocking to those who lived through them as the Immortalist Revolution is today.

You can live in the reality-tunnel imprinted upon you by environmental accident or you can choose your own. You can go through brain changes as radically bad as those of Patty Hearst and Rusty Calley, as transcendentally beautiful as those of Buddha and Jesus, as epistomologically revolutionary as those of Darwin and Einstein.

You can join those who have already entered the Immortalist Reality Tunnel, the Scientologist Reality-Tunnel or the Communist Reality-Tunnel.

"There are a lot of different realities going around these days," Abby Hoffman once said. Evolutionary acceleration is forcing us to the point where each will have to take responsibility for which reality we accept.

15 million Americans are waiting, trustingly, for the Space Brothers to come down in their UFOs and enforce World Peace.

The UFO is the, or an, extreme case. In general, *everything we see is inside our heads*!

This is demonstrated by the well-known optical diagram encountered in every high-school physics class:

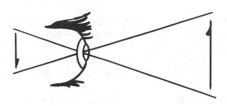

The light rays from the external object are reflected through the lens of the eye onto the retina, and reversed in the process. The brain obligingly interprets the picture, turning it right-side-up, and editing it in other ways more subtle.

What is true of vision is true of the other senses. What we know is what registers on the brain. This is the answer to the famous Zen Buddhist *koan* (riddle), "Who is the Master who makes the grass green?"

The brain, in the routine course of the before-mentioned 100,000,000 programs per minute, takes in, edits, orchestrates, organizes, packages, labels etc. all raw "existential" experience and classifies it according to the neurological Dewey Decimal System. This system varies from society to society; hence, cultural relativism -- what is "real" to the Eskimo is not quite the same as what is "real" to a New York taxi-driver.

To review: Each individual has a neurological system, or game, different from other members of the same society. In accord with Einstein's physical relativism, and anthropology's cultural relativism, we call this *neurological relativism.*

The vegetarian does not "see" (experience) meat on a rack in the butcher shop the same way the meat-eater sees it. The racist does not see a member of another race as, say, that person's parents do. More generally, as the Poet tells us. "The Fool sees not the same tree that the Wise Man sees."

Among the many editorial tasks of the brain, performed so rapidly and smoothly that we do not notice it, is the classification of the separate quanta of perception into "inside" and "outside." That this neat system does not accord with brute fact we learn from optics and neurology; that it can be abolished entirely, with great profit in terms of insight, we learn from the type of meta-programming experience called *dhyana* in the Hindu and Buddhist traditions.

Crowley says of the *dhyana* experience:

> In the course of our concentration we noticed that the contents of the mind at any moment consisted of two things, and no more: the (external) Object, variable, and the (internal) Subject, invariable, or apparently so. By success in dharana* the object has been made as invariable as the subject.
> Now the result of this is that the two become one. This phenomenon usually comes as a tremendous shock.

In our words, *"mind"* (whatever that is) *and its contents are functionally identical.* The usual system of classifying the contents as "me" (part of "mind") and not-"me" ("outside") can be abolished -- not just by meditation, but by certain well-known drugs -- and the unity of the field of perception is then recognized. We become Metaprogrammers.

This is what we might expect from the triumphs of field theory and general systems theory in sociology, anthropology, quantum theory etc. It still comes as a distinct shock when it is experienced, not just talked about. When "I" and "my world" (field of perception) become one, "I" am transformed utterly, as in "in a refiners' fire," as the mystics say.

This sounds a bit puzzling to the average person without experience in brain-change games. Try this illustration: Assuming you are reading this in your own home, look around the room. Note that everything in your field of vision -- furniture, paintings or posters on the walls, stereo set or absence of same, rugs, TV or not TV, etc. -- is, in a sense your *creation* or *co-creation.* You and/or your spouse or room-mate(s) *selected* everything that got into the room. You also *selected* or co-selected that particular room, out of the millions of rooms on this planet where you might otherwise live. The tunnel-reality of that room, then, in a very real sense has been *"created"* or *"manifested"* by you, out of a universe of infinite possibilities.

Of course, only the most fanatic Freudian or Buddhist mystic would claim your whole life history has been similarly "selected" by you. But, stop and think a moment: the life-history you *think* you have, the part that is stored in your brain as "memory," has certainly been selected. You can't even remember *everything* that happened in the last five minutes. If you try to be inwardly silent (passive; non-verbal) and notice everything happening in your field

*Silent meditation on one object for many weeks, like the Zen monk with the ox.

for *one* minute, you are overwhelmed by thousands of impressions that you cannot catalog and retain.

Conclusion: who you are, and what you think you are, is a creation edited and orchestrated by your brain.

Everybody you meet is an "artist" who has made a similar creation.

And these creations are, all of them, as diverse and idiosyncratic as the musical styles of Bach, Beethoven, Rock, Wagner, Vivaldi, Bizet, Orff, Chopin, John Cage, Soul, the Beatles, Harry James, Disco, Scotch folk-songs, African chants. . .

As for the universe "outside" you: of course, you didn't create that. But just *because you didn't create it, you can never know it. .* except approximately. What you do know, and consider "the universe outside" is another part of your brain, which has made of its circuits *a model* which you identify with the universe outside.

These models are as varied and miscellaneous as the paintings of Botticelli, Rembrandt, Van Gogh, Picasso, Paul Klee, Wyeth, Dali, Monet. . .

This the meaning of the notion that *mind and its contents are functionally identical.*

Consider the old folk-rhyme:

> **I saw a man upon the stair,**
> **A little man who wasn't there.**
> **He wasn't there again today;**
> **Gee, I wish he'd go away.**

This little man is a *semantic spook*; he exists only in the language, and yet once the language has invoked him *it almost seems to make sense* to wish he would go away.

Recent advances in semantics, semiotic, linguistic analysis, foundations of mathematics, logic, etc. have demonstrated that our conceptual field -- our symbolic environment -- is haunted by many such "spooks."

There are Empedoclean paradoxes, of which the classic is:

EVERYTHING IN THIS BOX IS FALSE

Theologians are vexed by questions like: Can an omnipotent God create a rock so heavy He Himself cannot lift it? (If he cannot, he is not omnipotent; and if he can, he is also not omnipotent.) Philosophers and physicists are still bothered by: what happened before Time began? Somebody is supposed to have remarked, "I'm glad I don't like cauliflower, because if I liked it, I'd eat it, and I hate the stuff." *Alice in Wonderland*, and any treatise on mathematical logic, will provide hundreds of examples of similar mind-benders.

A Zen saying sums it all up: "To think that I am not going to think of you anymore is still thinking of you. Let me then try not to think that I am not going to think of you."

Bertrand Russell and Alfred North Whitehead attempted to resolve all such conundrums with a mathematical proposition known as the Theory of Types. Unfortunately, it was quickly pointed out that either (a) the Theory of Types refers to itself, in which case it limits itself by its own terms, and does not solve all our semantic problems, or (b) the Theory of Types does not refer to itself, in which case there are propositions to which it does not refer, and it is again limited, and we are left with our problems.

These third-circuit perplexities are of more than technical logical and philosophical import. Many situations in real life take the form of our being haunted by our own semantic spooks. For instance, the popular novel, *Catch-22*, deals with a very real Empedoclean knot: the hero can escape from the war if he can prove his is crazy, but if he attempts to do this it will prove he is sane, since it is sane to escape a dangerous situation.

The logic of the dream-world of *Finnegans Wake* is not so far from real life, either. A patient, of German birth, at St. Elizabeth's hospital, would not walk through doors, explaining *"Da fressen mich die Turen."* (The doors will eat me.) This makes perfect sense phonetically, since it is identical in pronunciation with *"Da fressen mich die Tieren"* (The animals will eat me).

Word-magic? Schizophrenia? The average person, not a vegetarian, will respond positively to "tender juicy filet mignon" on the menu; but not to "a piece off of a dead castrated bull." But the two expressions mean the same thing.

We all tend to conjugate sentences in the manner caricatured by Bertrand Russell: "I am firm. You are obstinate. He is a pig-headed fool." ("I am daring and original. You are pretentious.

She stinks." "I am flexible. You bend with the wind. They're a bunch of opportunists.")

The magic of poetry creates "real toads in imaginary gardens," it has been said. When Robert Burns writes:

> The wan moon is setting behind the white wave
> And Time is setting with me, oh

it is hard not to feel that the abstraction "time" has become as real as the physical moon and wave -- or the little man upon the stair.

Consider the following table:

COLUMN I	COLUMN II
Nigger-loving busy body	Civil libertarian
Smutty book	Realistic Novel
Daring and original theory	Wild and implausible speculation
Sexist enterprise	Dealer in rare and exotic art
Wooly-headed liberal	Passionate humanitarian
Sound, sensible economics	Stingy, tight-assed idea

Any phrase in column I can describe persons or events that might very well be described, by a different speaker, with the corresponding phrase in column II. Now the reader may feel that some of the phrases above are so pejorative, so loaded with prejudice, that only the most ignorant or bigoted would use them; but that is irrelevant. What needs to be noted is that it is *easy* to see the bias in somebody else's semantic maps, but not so easy to see the bias in one's own semantic reality-tunnel. If the reader were born in Arkansas in the 1920s, item 1 in Column I might seem the natural, accurate, normal way to refer to the first NAACP worker to appear and try to organized the Blacks.

These matters are symbolic, but more than linguistic. For example, the proverbial Englishman who dressed for dinner every night in his lonely tropical hut was no fool. He was keeping *an English third-circuit reality bubble* around him, to avoid becoming engulfed in the reality-bubble of the natives.

It only takes a few weeks in prison to become "a convict," whatever your definition of yourself was before, it only takes a few weeks in the Army to become a "soldier."

These remarks are another elucidation of our earlier statement that *mind and its contents are functionally identical.* The symbolizing process is such that, once set in motion, it is virtually impossible (without subtle neurological know-how) to escape from a reality-tunnel one has created for oneself or had foisted upon one by the environment.

Kurt Saxon is the author of *The Poor Man's James Bond,* a manual that tells you everything you could ever want to know about practical techniques of murder and mayhem, *The Survivor,* a four-volume extension of the same libretto, telling where to acquire any possible type of weapon, *Root Rot,* a diatribe against Alex Haley for implying that slavery was unfair to Black people, and several similar books. Mr. Saxon does not get reviewed in the Liberal magazines that decide which authors are important, but he has a wide readership among the Apocalyptical sects of the right-wing end of the political spectrum.

Mr. Saxon believes, and insists vehemently, that the United States will be destroyed almost totally by 1982. This is because the government has driven the "competents" out of business by excessive taxation and has subsidized 30 million "incompetents" on Welfare and another 30 million "incompetents" on Social Security. This country has thus become, Saxon says, "a Disneyland for dummies."

By 1982, Saxon avers, the whole economy will collapse. "Millions of taxpayers will be unemployed. . .Millions who are now on Valium or other tranquilizers will go insane when they cannot get more. . .Drug addicts (will) swarm over pharmacies looking for dope, ruining everything they don't steal. . ." We will be helpless against Russian attack because "our politicians have so devoted themselves to nurturing. . .incompetent dependents that further industrialization to put our nation on a war footing will be unaffordable. Even if it were not, our present union-spoiled and demanding work force cannot be expected to perform the way

212

our parents did in the war plants of the late '30s and early '40s."

The only solution, Saxon informs us, is to buy farms, order his books on how to kill people efficiently, and stockpile every type of weaponry, to fight off the "drooling imbeciles and parasites" who will flee the doomed cities and try to steal your crops.

Mr. Saxon believes that these are *objective predictions* based on hard *"laws"* of sociology and economics which he learned from the writings of Ms. Ayn Rand. He does not believe that this apocalyptical reality tunnel in which he lives is in any way an *artistic creation* expressing his own emotional anxieties and hostilities.

John White believes that the earth will shift on its axis some-time before 1999. There will be "massive loss of life" and civiliza-tion will be almost totally destroyed. The only hope you have, he says, is to retreat to a farm (a la Mr. Saxon) where you will probably be wiped out anyway but have some advantage over city-people in that you won't have tall buildings falling on you when the Pole Shift sets off earthquakes everywhere.

Mr. White believes that these are *objective* predictions based on eternal *"laws"* of *karma* which he learned from various occult-ists and gurus. He does not believe that the apocalyptical reality-tunnel in which he lives is in any way an *artistic creation* expressing his own emotional anxieties and hostilities.

Mr. White also believes that many UFOs are actually demons, and that after the Pole Shift kills us off, most of us will go to "Hell," which is not eternal, fortunately, but only "timeless."

If we confront the world without ideas we see only a muddle, the formless void that existed before "God" (intellect) started to create a universe (a system) in Genesis.

Once we become the "image of God" by making our own universe, we have a model of the muddle. The model is very convenient -- we could not be human without it -- but it is also very misleading whenever we forget that we have created it.

None of the reality-models discussed in this chapter, however bizarre they may seem to some readers, are any more arbitrary than the official reality-model known as consensus-reality, which is a statistical average and not nearly consensual as it seems. Travel 100 miles in any direction, and the consensus begins to

crumble. Travel 1000 miles and very little consensus is left. . .
"The peoples of the earth are islands," said the late Clement Atlee, "shouting at each other over oceans of misunderstanding." Each island is a separate reality-tunnel created by (a) our culture, (b) our sub-culture and (c) by the myth-maker or *artist* in each of us who is the adamantine individuality that makes you and me unique human selves not replicable units like the ants in a hive.

Robert Anton Wilson is the author of *Cosmic Trigger, Schrödinger's Cat, Sex and Drugs* and several other books. Like Mr. Saxon and Mr. White, Wilson does not get reviewed in the Liberal magazines that decide which authors are important, but he has a wide readership among science-fiction fans, political Libertarians and veterans of the Consciousness Revolution.

Dr. Wilson believes that life extension techniques and intelligence raising drugs will be discovered in this decade, and will be widely available by 1995. Less radical than Dr. Silverstein, Wilson does not expect immortality to be achieved until the middle of the next century -- but he expects life-extension drugs will keep him around until then.

Dr. Wilson expects most of humanity will have migrated off Earth into space cities by 2028. He expects that with higher intelligence and longer lives than past humanity, these post-terrestrials will gradually become Superhuman by comparison with our historical average.

Wilson believes that these are good guesses based on scientific probabilities, but he does not think there are any hard economic or karmic *laws* guaranteeing them. He recognizes that this reality-tunnel was generated by his own brain, that he is the *artist* who created it, and that it expresses his own hopes and desires, as well as scientific probabilities. It is, he knows, the reality-tunnel that keeps him happy, creative, busy and full of zest for life.

He doesn't think it is any crazier than anybody else's reality-tunnel, and he claims it is a lot more fun than any other.

EXERCIZES

1. Using the four circuit model, try to guess which specific imprints created Mr. Saxon's reality-tunnel.
2. Apply the same analysis to Mr. White and Dr. Wilson.

3. Apply the same analysis to Jesus, Hitler, Walt Whitman and your own father and mother.

4. Write a criticism of this chapter from the viewpoint of Christian Fundamentalism.

CHAPTER SIXTEEN

THE SNAFU PRINCIPLE

. . .the peculiar nature of the game. . .makes it
impossible for [participants] to stop the game
once it is under way. Such situations we label
games without end.

Watzlawick, Beavin, Jackson,
Pragmatics of Human Communication

DOMINANCE
"HERRENMORAL"

SUBMISSION
"SKLAVMORAL"

This is second circuit neuro-politics

They shall come to know good.
James Joyce, Finnegans Wake

Mammalian sociobiology, rooted in the antique neural circuits of the old brain, contains many factors opposing the evolution of domesticated primates into true freedom and objective intelligence.

The chief of these "reactionary" factors was described in my novel *Illuminatus!* as the Snafu Principle or Celine's Law. It holds that *communication is only possible between equals.*

This was an over-simplification for fictional (satirical) purposes. More precisely, this proposed "law" would read:

Adequate communication flows freely between equals. Communication between non-equals is warped and distorted by second-circuit Domination and Submission rituals perpetuating communication jam and a Game Without End.

Political power, as a typical alpha male once said, grows out of the barrel of a gun. This is metaphorically as well as literally true. The "gun" may be symbolic and fairly abstract, consisting of ritualized social expectations ("Don't talk back to your father") or concrete in a non-violent but deadly way, e.g. the capacity to remove bio-survival necessities by cutting off the ticket supply in a Capitalist society ("One more word and I'll fire you, Bumstead!").

Under the primate second-circuit sociobiological rules, everybody tends to lie a little, to flatter or to evade displeasure, when exchanging signals with those above them in the pack-hierarchy.

Every authoritarian structure can be visualized as a pyramid with an eye on the top. This is the typical flow-chart of any government, any corporation, any Army, any bureaucracy, any mammalian pack. On each rung, participants bear *a burden of nescience* in relation to those above them. That is, they must be very, very careful that the natural sensory activities of being conscious organisms -- the acts of seeing, hearing, smelling, drawing inferences from perception, etc. -- are in *accord with the reality-tunnel of those above them*. This is absolutely vital; pack status (and "job security") depends on it. It is much less important -- a luxury that can easily be discarded -- that these perceptions be *in accord with objective fact*.

For instance, in the F.B.I. under J. Edgar Hoover, the agent had to develop a capacity to see godless communists everywhere. Any agent whose perceptions indicated that there were actually very few godless communists in this country at that time would experience *cognitive dissonance* -- his or her reality-tunnel was at variance with the "offical" reality-tunnel of the pyramid. To talk about such perceptions at all would be to invite suspicions of eccentricity, intellectual wiseacreing or of being oneself a godless communist. The same would apply to a Dominican inquisitor in the middle ages who lacked the capacity to "see" witches everywhere. In such authoritarian situations, it is important to see what the Top Dogs (alpha males) see; it is inconvenient, and possibly dangerous to see what is objectively happening.

But this leads to an equal and opposite *burden of omniscience* upon those at the top, in the eye of the pyramid. All that is forbidden to those at the bottom -- the conscious activities of perception and evaluation -- is demanded of the Power Elite, the master class. *They must attempt to do the seeing, hearing, smelling, etc. and all the thinking and evaluating* for the whole pyramid.

But a man with a gun (the power to punish) is told only what the target thinks will not cause him to pull the trigger (write the pink slip, order the court-martial). The elite, with their *burden of omniscience*, face the underlings, with their *burden of nescience*, and receive only the feedback consistent with their own preconceived notions and reality-tunnels. The burden of omniscience becomes, over time, another and more complex burden of nescience. Nobody really knows anything anymore, or if they do, they are careful to hide the fact. The burden of nescience becomes omnipresent. More and more of sensory experience becomes unspeakable.

As Paul Watzlawick notes, that which is objectively repressed (unspeakable) soon becomes subjectively repressed (unthinkable). Nobody likes to feel like a coward and a liar constantly. *It is easier to cease to notice where the official tunnel-reality differs from existential fact.* Thus SNAFU accelerates and *rigiditus bureaucraticus* sets in -- the last stage before all brain activity ceases and the pyramid is clinically dead as an intellectual entity.

We also propose that "national security" is another semantic spook, an Empedoclean knot; that the search for national security is the chief cause of national insecurity and a potent anti-intelligence mechanism.

As Leary writes:

> **Secrecy is the original sin. Fig leaf in the Garden of Eden. The basic crime against love. . .The purpose of life is to receive, synthesize and transmit energy. Communication fusion is the goal of life. Any star can tell you that. Communication is love. Secrecy, witholding the signal, hoarding, hiding, covering up the light is motivated by shame and fear.**
>
> **As so often happens, the right wing is half right for the wrong reasons. They say primly: if you have done nothing wrong, you have no fear of being bugged. Exactly. But the logic goes both ways. Then F.B.I. files, C.I.A. dossiers, White House conversations should be open to all. Let everything hang open. Let government be totally visible. The last, the very last people to hide their actions should be the police and the government.**

What my eminent colleague states so poetically can be stated more functionally as follows:

Every secret police agency must be monitored by an elite corps or secret-police-of-the-second-order. This is because (1) Infiltration of the secret police, for purposes of subversion, will always be a prime goal of both internal subversives and hostile foreign powers. (2) Secret police agencies acquire fantastic capacities to blackmail and intimidate others, in and out of government. Stalin executed three chiefs of the secret police in a row, because of this danger. As Nixon so wistfully said in a Watergate transcript, "Well, Hoover performed. He would have fought. That was the point. He would have defied a few people. He would have scared them to death. *He had a file on everybody."* (Italics added.) Thus, those who employ secret police agencies *must* monitor them, to be sure they are not acquiring too much power.

Here a sinister infinite regress enters the game. Any elite second order police must be, also. subject to infiltration, or to acquiring "too much power" in the opinion of its masters. And so it, too, must be monitored, by a secret-police-of-the-third-order.

In brief, once a government has *n* orders of secret police spying on each other, all are potentially suspect, and to be safe a secret police of order *n plus 1* must be created. And so on, forever.

In practise, of course, this cannot regress to mathematical infinity, but only to the point where every citizen, is spying on every other citizen or until the funding runs out.

National Security, in practise, must always fall short of the logically Empedoclean infinite regress it requires for perfect "security." In that gap between the ideal of "One Nation under surveillance with wire taps and mail covers for all," and the strictly limited real situation of finite resources and finite funding, there is ample encouragement for paranoias of all sorts to flourish, both among the citizens and among the police.

THE BURDEN OF OMNISCIENCE

or, why you can't reach the Court or the Castle in Kafka's allegories

Thus, the U.S.S.R. after 62 years of Marxist secret police games has reached the point where the alpha males are terrified of *painters and poets.*

In spying-and-hiding transactions, worry leads to more worry and suspicion leads to more suspicion. The very act of participating, however unwillingly, in the secret police game -- even as victim, or citizen being monitored -- will eventually produce all the classic symptoms of clinical paranoia.

The agent knows who he is spying on, but he never knows who is spying on him. Could it be his wife, his mistress, his secretary, the newsboy, the Good Humor man?

If there is a secret police at all, in any nation, *every branch and department of government,* and institutions which are not even admitted to be parts of government, *becomes suspect in the eyes of cautious and intelligent people as a possible front for, or tunnel to, the secret police.* That is, the more shrewd will recognize that something bearing the label of H.E.W. or even International Silicon and Pencil might actually be the C.I.A. or N.S.A. in disguise.

In such a deception network, conspiracy theories proliferate. Rumor is necessary, it has been found, when people cannot find "offical" news sources that can be trusted to tell them what is really going on. The present author, having worked in the civil rights movement, the anti-war movement, the legalize-pot movement and other dissident causes, has repeatedly been approached by friend A with dire warnings that friend B is almost certainly a secret police agent, only to be told later and independently by friend C that friend A is a secret police agent. It requires delicate neurological know-how to keep one's sense of humor in the secret police matrix.

The more omnipresent the secret police, the more likely it is that intelligent men and women will regard the government with fear and loathing.

The government, on discovering that growing numbers of citizens regard it with fear and loathing, will increase the size and powers of the secret police, to protect itself.

The infinite regress again appears.

SUSPICION LEADS TO MORE SUSPICION

The only alternative was suggested sarcastically by playwright Bert Brecht (who was hounded by U.S. secret police as a communist and by East German secret police, later, as not sufficiently communist). "If the government doesn't trust the people," Brecht asked innocently, "why doesn't it dissolve them and elect a new people?" No way has yet been invented to elect a new people, so the government will instead spy on the existing people with increased vigor.

Every secret police organization is engaged in both the *collection of information* and the *production of misinformation,* euphemistically called "disinformation." That is, you score points in the secret police game both by hoarding signals (information units) -- hiding facts from competitors -- and by foisting false signals (fake information units) on the other players. This creates the situation I call Optimum SNAFU, in which every player has rational (not neurotic) reasons for suspecting that each and all may be trying to deceive him, gull him, con him, dupe him and generally misinform him. As Henry Kissinger is alleged to have said, anybody in Washington who isn't paranoid must be crazy.

Maybe the UFOs really exist objectively -- or maybe the whole UFO phenomenon is a cover for a secret police disinformation ploy. Maybe there are Black Holes where space and time implode -- or maybe Black Holes were invented to befuddle Russian scientists and send them into "little man who wasn't there" semantic spookery. Maybe Jimmy Carter really exists -- or maybe he is, as *National Lampoon* once claimed, an actor named Sidney Goldfarb trained to project an attractive down-home "image." Perhaps only three alpha males at the top of the National Security pyramid really know the answers to these questions -- or perhaps these three are being deceived by certain subordinates, as Lyndon Johnson was deceived about Vietnam by the C.I.A.

Such is the neurosociological "logic" of a Disinformation Matrix. It is, as Paul Watzlawik has demonstrated, the logic of schizophrenia.

Less than ten years after the secret police game was established here by the National Security Act of 1948, the books of Dr. Wilhelm Reich were burned in a New York incinerator by government order. This was a shocking sight to some of us, who remembered that we had recently fought a long war against Nazi Germany for, among other things, their crime "against civilization" of burning books. Shortly thereafter, Dr. William Ivy, former head of a department at Chicago Medical School, was subjected to ten years of legal harassment for espousing a radical cancer cure. More recently, Dr. Timothy Leary was sentenced to 38 years imprisonment for espousing controversial ideas about neurotransmitter chemicals and re-imprinting the nervous system. Now there is a war on against laetrile.

It does not matter whether any or all of these "heretics" were right or wrong. Scientific truth is only determined after a generation or more of research; it is not determined by throwing the dissenters in prison or burning their books. The point is that the secret police game immediately creates the social context for a return to the mechanisms of the Holy Inquisition.

The intelligence of the whole society -- the communication networks through which information is received, decoded and transmitted -- is the first casualty.

"I feel great and I send fraternal greetings to Dr. Andrei Sakharov in Russia," said Dr. Leary on emerging from prison, registering the fact that the mechanisms of the police state are the same everywhere, as are the myths that protect them. "Good Russians" believe Dr. Sakharov is a half-crazed alcoholic, just as "Good Americans" believe Dr. Leary is a half-crazed dope-fiend.

I once proposed in a magazine article that the UFO is caused by some unusual electro-magnetic or gravitational field fluctuation; and that this geophysical anomaly creates (a) real energy disturbances -- jumping furniture, electrical failures, ball-lightning making odd lights in the sky, etc. and (b) disturbance in the brain functioning of animals and humans in the afflicted area, causing the well-documented animal panics and the rather obvious human hallucinations occurring in such areas.

Statistical support for this theory will be found in Persinger and Lafeniere who have run computer-analyses of common patterns in 1,242 UFO cases and 4,818 other "abnormal" reports "poltergeists," "teleportations," "miracles" and "mysteries" of all sorts. This data demonstrates that both UFOs and other energy anomalies tend to cluster along earthquake faults with some peaking before earthquakes. Persinger and Lafreniere also suggest that the geophysical forces at work create both real oddities (jumping furniture, etc.) and hallucinations, so that it is a job of nice and exquisite discrimination to attempt to find out what was really going on.

It has also been proposed, by the learned Dr. Jacques Vallee, astronomer, cyberneticist and physicist, that the UFO phenomenon is being created by a secret police agency as an elaborate "cover" for a complex disinformation system.

A combined Wilson-Persinger-Lafreniere-Vallee theory, probably fitting more of the data than the separate theories, would suggest that the UFO phenomenon is the synergetic product of some geophysical oddity which created weird energy fluctuations and brain-change experiences in humans on the scene, *and* is being manipulated after the fact by one or more "intelligence" agencies, or by groups even more esoteric.

Consider this scenario:

Something weird happens. Assume that it is the geophysical abnormality and brain-change trauma we posit, but grant also that it might be the alien spaceship beloved by folk-myth. The following events are equally likely, whatever the weirdity "really was."

As soon as the witnesses start talking, All Interested Parties converge on the area. Intelligence Agent Moe comes to *conceal* evidence that it might have been a spaceship -- that is the policy of his agency, for their own reasons. Intelligence Agent Joe also arrives to plant evidence that it *was* a spaceship -- that is the policy of his agency, since they are doing just what Dr. Vallee suspects. (The British Double Cross Bureau, in World War II, engaged in equally complex and absurdist dramas, seemingly totally unrelated to their actual work, but serving as disinformation screens for that work.) Philip Klass and other Skeptics arrive, too, trying to reduce *everything* to "hallucination," even if eyes are burned, cars wrecked, etc. The Space Freaks, who may or may not be infiltrated by associates of Intelligence Agent Joe, are soon there, too, to get the facts to fit their Benign Space Brothers reality-tunnel. Various occultists are there, too, to fit it all into their own mythos of angelology, demonology, etc.

What we are saying is that every conspiracy regards itself as an affinity group -- men and women who share the same goals and work together well. When you and I do it, it is just an affinity group.

When that gang over there does it, it is a damnable conspiracy. True conspiracy does exist when a group conceals evidence, spreads deliberate misinformation and coerces or terrorizes witnesses. Any affinity group approaches such behavior to the extent that members reinforce each other's participation in the group reality-tunnel, especially concerning such crucial epistemological matters as what is important enough to notice *and discuss,* as against what is trivial and better ignored. How coercive do we have to be to intimidate witnesses? Most people, as our Snafu Principle explains, are easily led to reporting what an Authority Figure wants to hear.

But let us consider the UFO syndrome further, as illustrating the whole spectrum of brain-change, and brain-programming.

UFO contactees frequently show positive *neurosomatic turn on,* the bliss-out experience; some even become faith-healers or leaders of occultist groups. Others show negative neurosomatic effects -- light is unbearable, as in schizophrenia, anxiety attacks may require hospitalization, etc.

Metaprogramming consciousness (the ability to choose between alternative reality-tunnels) is also reported, in crude metaphors about "parallel universes," "other realities," occultish jargon.

Neurogenetic (Jungian "collective unconscious") visions are common, ranging from demons, hairy dwarfs etc. to the Space Goddess or Lady of the Stars of ancient and Catholic iconography.

Even metaphysiological (quantum-level) experience is reported in the UFO literature, ranging from trans-time trips and "out-of-body experiences" to seeming, or alleged, teleportations.

It must be emphasized most strongly that both positive and negative visions on all these circuits are common in UFOlogy. It seems that if the Programmers mean us well, they are accidentally doing ill to many: and if they mean us ill, as Dr. Vallee thinks, they are accidentally doing well to some of us. But this is true of all brain-change technology.

It seems that Vallee's monistic conspiracy theory is inadequate, as monistic conspiracy theories are inadequate in politics. It is more likely that the UFO experience, like the other brain-change experiences we have studied, are sometimes spontaneous and sometimes programmed; and that *there are rival gangs of programmers with radically different goals in mind for humanity.*

When Dr. Leary and I first published a neurological analysis of the Patty Hearst case in OUI magazine, the editors introduced it with a dramatic headline:

The fight for Patty Hearst's mind is the overture to a worldwide battle for the control of consciousness.

Not quite. The Hearst case would more appropriately be considered a bar near the end of the second movement of the Mind War symphony. The *first movement* was the primitive neuroscience of ancient and medieval tyrants who acquired a great deal of pragmatic know-how about the effects of isolation, terror and intimidation; and of shamans and occultists who learned how neuro-chemicals can alter perceived reality-tunnels. The *second movement* began with modern psychology, with Freud, Pavlov, Jung, Skinner etc., climaxing with the LSD revolution and the discovery by millions that reality-tunnels could be radically mutated -- temporarily and sometimes permanently -- by neuro-chemistry.

The *third movement* is the growingly obvious warfare between those who would program all of us, and those of us who wish to become our own metaprogrammers.

EXERCIZES

1. Start collecting evidence that your phone is bugged.

2. Everybody gets a letter occasionally that is slightly damaged. Assume that somebody is opening your mail and clumsily resealing it.

3. Look around for evidence that your co-workers or neighbors think you're a bit queer and are planning to have you committed to a mental hospital.

4. Try living a whole week with the program, "Everybody likes me and tries to help me achieve all of my goals."

5. Try living a whole month with the program, "I have chosen to be aware of this particular reality."

6. Try living a day with the program "I am God playing at being a human being. I created every reality I notice." Assume that "GOD" is the answer to Da Free John's question, "Who is the one who is living you now?"

7. Try living forever with the metaprogram, "Everything works out more perfectly than I plan it."

230

CHAPTER SEVENTEEN

QUANTUM EVOLUTION

What is man? A bridge between the ape and the Superman -- a bridge over an abyss.

F.W. Nietzsche, Thus Spake Zarathustra

Another persepective on domesticated primate evolution is provided by Alvin Toffler's *The Third Wave.*

For convenience Toffler reduces the muddle of human history into a model of three waves. It would be more accurate to refer to these "waves" as quantum jumps in energy-coherence level.

The First Wave, Toffler says, took *milleniums* to occur, but it finally transformed the larger part of humanity from the tribal stage (simple hunting-gathering primates) to the stage of large-scale agricultural-feudal civilizations.

The Second Wave came much faster and, in a few *centuries*, transformed almost all of humanity from feudal-agricultural-cottage economy to industrial-urban-market economy.

The Third Wave, Toffler says, continues the trend toward acceleration and will happen in only a few *decades,* "the information explosion," "the post industrial economy," etc.

Each wave is faster, by a factor of 10, than the previous wave. And each wave is more *total* in that it changes more people, changes them more completely, and in the process transforms our concept of human nature and human society.

Each wave that Toffler describes can be considered a new quantum state, with energy levels and reality-dimensions lacking in the previous state and totally unpredictable from the previous state.

The First Wave mutated tribal men and women into serfs (or into Lords and Ladies). It created a whole new social manifold that is so subtle and pervasive that anthropologists and sociologists can spend years studying its invisible aspects. And yet this transformation is so enormous that it is also visible to the most untrained eyes: you can't confuse a tribal human with a feudal human anymore than you can confuse a dog with a donkey.

So, too, the Second Wave created what Toffler wittily calls "indust-reality," manifesting as industrial men and women who are visibly, tangibly, as different from feudal or tribal humans as dolphins are from rose bushes or armadillos.

The Third Wave, which began when Shannon and Wiener defined *information* and Von Neumann designed the first programmable computer, is well under way already. Many experts agree that home computers will be as common as TV sets by the mid-1980s. This transformation, again, will be *total*: it will create a whole new "man." a new "woman," a new "child," a new "self," new "society," a new concept of "work" and "energy" and "reality," etc.

The average Man or Woman of 1983 will be as obsolete in 2003 as the medieval serf is now. What we consider normal jobs, normal social roles, normal "humanity" will be as archaic as a horde of alchemists, smithies, Town Criers, courtiers and barber-surgeons arriving in our midst today.

Of course, Toffler does not claim that the computer is the *whole* of the Third Wave, but merely that it is the synecdoche or paradigm of what is happening. In this sense, the factory was the synecdoche of the Second Wave. It was not merely the agent by which "indust-reality" spread across the world and multiplied our collective wealth (and illth); it also became the model for everything else. Our schools are mini-factories or models of factories because their main job was, when they were founded, to prepare people for factory work. The schools, in fact, were necessary because, while feudalism does not require literacy of the masses, industrialism does. Similarly, offices were modeled on factories, and kept factory-hours, even when this had little or nothing to do with how the offices could most efficiently be managed. And in general, "indust-reality," the reality of the industrial age, moved everybody into the robot lockstep of the factory system.*

"Indust-reality" is still so pervasive that it is, as McLuhan noted, mostly invisible. For instance, the feudal age never progressed beyond chamber music -- trios, quartets etc. The modern symphony, with its huge orchestra, its Promethean themes, its god-like conductor ("capitalist"), its concert-master (foreman), its string section moving in harmony with its brass section, etc. is a beautiful artistic expression of modes of mass human organization appearing usually in less beautiful forms in the factory assembly-line. (The factory also demanded cities -- massive concentrations of labor in one place -- which made the symphony economically possible. The aristocrat could not afford, and/or could not conceive, keeping more than the very few musicians necessary for chamber music.)

*A free-lance writer can obviously work *any* hours, but the very successful (and very excellent) John D. MacDonald said in a recent interview that he always writes from nine to five, because it seems "natural" to him. The factory time-clock has gotten into MacDonald's neurons. The present author, after 20 years in factory-like offices, works any hours of the day or night when "the spirit" moves him, but *never* starts at nine or stops at five, to avoid relapsing into the habits of his past.

Beethoven's "cosmic optimism" not only expresses the Age of Reason out of which indust-reality emerged; the very orchestras he wrote for were paradigms of industrial styles of organization. Of course, industrialism (the Second Wave) produced much illth along with its new wealth; and most of the wealth was ex-(or ap)-propriated by a minority. However much this may pain socialists, it was inevitable in a domesticated primate species. A few alpha males can always see their own advantage more clearly than the majority can see their collective interest.

Nonetheless, as indust-reality has spread, socialism has followed in its wake. Whether the reader likes this or not (and the author, being up-front about his prejudices, admits that he does not like it), this also is inevitable. When huge wealth is palpably being created in vaster accumulations than ever before in history, there is sure to be increased grumbling against the alpha males, and more attempts to seize what they have selfishly ap-(or ex)-propriated. Even among baboons this pattern has been observed: the alpha male who is too obnoxious gets beaten up by a coalition of younger males and thrown out of the pack to forage alone.

Neither capitalist indust-reality nor socialist indust-reality have been able to give humanity what most of us really want: liberty *and* justice, freedom *and* the abolition of poverty, continued growth *and* continued security. In looking at capitalism vs. socialism, we are always confronted with a dilemma, not a choice.

The Third Wave can, and will, transcend this problem within industrialism. The Third Wave will be neither capitalist nor socialist, nor some milkwater blend of the two. It will demand a whole new economy, just as feudalism created an economy unknown to tribal humanity and industrialism created the two competing economies of capitalism and socialism, both unguessed and unpredictable from the perspective of the feudal stage.

In 1977, Dr. Ilya Prigogine won the Nobel prize in physical chemistry.

Perhaps he should have won a Nobel prize for intelligent optimism.

Dr. Prigogine's work deals with the processes we have been discussing -- the emergence of negative entropy (coherent order) out of stochastic processes -- but he has taken a giant leap beyond the pioneering insights of Schrödinger, Weiner, Shannon and Bateson.

Any organized system, according to Prigogine, exists in dynamic tension between entropy and negentrophy, between chaos and information. The more complex the system, the greater is its *instability*. Prigogine demonstrated this mathematically, but in everyday terms, what he means is that, for instance, it is easier to lead two children through a department store than twenty children. Or: A toothpick "house" of 101 pieces is less stable than a smaller toothpick "house" of 10 pieces.

Instability is not always bad: in fact, it is absolutely necessary for evolution to occur. Insect societies are highly stable and have not evolved at all in several million years. Human societies are highly unstable and are in continuous evolution.

Prigogine demonstrates the evolutionary value of instability by his concept of the *"dissipative structure."*

A dissipative structure is highly complex and therefore highly unstable. The more complex it is, the more unstable it is, mathematically, certainly; and the more unstable, the more likely it is to change -- to evolve.

All dissipative structures are teetering, perpetually, between self-destruction and re-organization on a higher level of informaton (coherence).

If that sounds grim, it isn't really. Prigogine's math is highly optimistic, He shows that the more complex structures -- such as our world-round human society today, midway between Second Wave indust-reality and the emerging Third Wave -- are mathematically more likely, *much more likely,* to "dissipate" into higher coherence than into self-destruction.

In other words, in the intellectual conflict between Utopians and Dystopians, the mathematical odds actually are on the side of Utopians. Our human world is so information-rich (coherent) that it is almost certain to "collapse" into even higher coherence, not into chaos and self-destruction.

Prigogine is the mathematical demonstration of McLuhan's intuition that many seeming symptoms of *breakdown* are actually harbingers of *breakthrough.*

A note to confirmed pessimists: Prigogine's analysis is based on probability-theory and, hence, is not *certain.* Thus, if you have found these lyrical pages unduly alarming, take comfort in the thought that, although human success is highly probable, there is still a small chance that we can blow ourselves up or that your favorite apocalyptic scenarios might still occur, despite the general trend toward higher coherence and higher intelligence.

Meanwhile, of course, even if humanity seems condemned to overall success, you can still mess up your personal life. Nothing in this book is an attempt to prevent the really resolute misery-addicts from continuing their pursuit of frustration and failure.

The latest cosmological evidence indicates that our sun and its planets, including Earth, condensed out of a cloud of galactic dust and gas about five or six billion years ago.

It appears that the first forms of unicellular life -- the first dawnings of Circuit I bio-survival "consciousness" -- appeared about 3.4 billion years ago.

Vertebrates began to appear -- with Circuit II emotional-territorial consciousness -- about .5 billion years ago (500 million years ago).

The emergence of Circuit III human intelligence - language and "thought" -- seems to have begun about 100,000 years ago. The fully human domesticated primate, Homo Sapiens, with Circuit IV "moral" consciousness may be about 30 thousand years old, or even more recent. Circuits V-VIII have appeared within historical times.

All of these figures are subject to revision as science advances, but the rough proportions between them are not likely to be changed much, and these *proportions* are staggering.

As has often been pointed out, if we condense this evolutionary scenario into a 24-hour day, beginning at midnight, life itself does not appear until a little before noon, and all of human history (from the grunting, club-wielding apemen of Africa to Neil Armstrong setting foot on the moon) occurs in *the last half of the last second* before midnight strikes again and the day ends.

This model is misleading in that it assumes the present is an "end," which is highly unlikely. Even without Space Migration, the lifespan of earth's biosphere is expected to be somewhere between 10 and 15 billion years more, before the Sun ceases to support life here. Taking the Sun's expected lifespan of about 20 billion years as our model to be mapped onto a single day, we find that it's now around eight in the morning. Life has been mostly unconscious until now -- operating on auto-pilot, as it were -- but in the last million years (the last few seconds on this model) signs of consciousness and Awakening are beginning to appear.

"The universe is so constructed as to be able to see itself," Spencer Brown once noted. The emergence of the neurosomatic, neurogenetic and metaprogramming circuits is the universe's way of "seeing itself" ever more clearly and totally, to decide where it is going.

Dr. Issac Asimov notes in his *Genetic Code* that there seems to be a 60-year cycle between the first understanding of a new scientific principle and *the transformation of the world by that principle.*

For instance, Oersted discovered electromagnetic equivalence -- the fact that electricity can be converted to magnetism, and magnetism to electricity -- in 1820. Sixty years later, in 1880, electrical generators were in wide use and the Industrial Revolution had peaked; the telegraph and telephone were already invented, and our age of Mass Communication was dawning.

Similarly, in 1883, Thomas Edison first noted the so-called "Edison effect" -- the key to electronic, as distinct from electrical, engineering. 60 years later, in 1943, electronic technology was appearing everywhere; its primitive form in the entertainment sphere, radio, had enjoyed a 20-year triumph and was about to be phased out by television.

In 1896, Becquerel noted the radioactivity of uranium. Sixty years later, two cities had been destroyed by atomic bombs and nuclear plants were beginning to be built. (This was a contribution to illth, not wealth.)

In 1903, the Wright Brothers got their monoplane off the ground for a few minutes. Sixty years later, in 1963, jetliners carrying over 100 passengers were normal.

Assuming, gambling, guesstimating that this 60-year cycle is normal, we can predict:

Shannon and Weiner created the mathematical foundations of cybernetics in 1948. Sixty years later, in 2008, cybernetization of the world, as complete as the electrification of the 19th Century, will have jumped us to a new energy-level, a new social reality, as Toffler predicts.

Hoffman discovered LSD and the chemical control of consciousness in 1943. Sixty years later, in 2003, every alteration in consciousness imaginable will be possible by ingesting the proper chemicals.

McKay had the first success in expanding life-span of laboratory rats in 1938. Sixty years later, in 1998, immortality pills may be routinely available in all drugstores.

DNA was identified in 1944. Sixty years later, in 2004, every type of genetic engineering should be as routine as electronic engineering is today.

All of these estimates are probably conservative, since they assume Asimov's 60-year cycle as normal, and every field of technology is actually accelerating faster all the time. We would be wiser to divide each estimate by half and assume most of these changes will occur in the next ten years -- before the 1980s are over.

The latest attempt to estimate the rate of information acceleration -- the manifestation of coherence -- was made by French economist Georges Anderla for the Organization for Economic Cooperation and Development (OECD) in 1973.

Anderla arbitrarily assumed that all the bits of information possessed by humanity at the beginning of the Christian Era (1 A.D.) could be considered his unit of measurement. He made that information pool one unit in our fund of knowledge.

It took until 1500 A.D., Anderla discovered, for the accumulation of bits of information to add up to two units in our "fund."

It required only 250 years more (to 1750) for our bank of knowledge to double again, to four units.

The next doubling took 150 years and by 1900 humanity had 8 units in its information capital account.

The next doubling took only 50 years and by 1950 we had 16 units.

The next doubling took only 10 years and by 1960 we had 32 units.

The next doubling took seven years and by 1967 we had 64 units. (This was coincidentally the height of the *first* Youth Revolution, when reality maps began breaking down everywhere on the planet and wild new maps were hurtling at us from all directions.)

In the next six year period (1967-1973), our intellectual bank

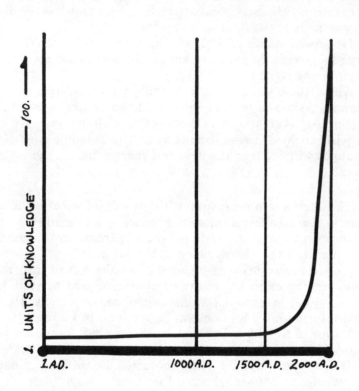

THE INFORMATION EXPLOSION

account again doubled, to 128 units. At this point, Anderla completed his study.

Dr. Alvin Silverstein has estimated that, if Anderla's graph is projected ahead seventy years from now (1980-2050) human knowledge should increase a *millionfold*. That is, we should have 128,000,000 times more knowledge than we had in the year of Jesus' birth.

Longevity drugs will probably arrive in time for you to live through the biggest evolutionary quantum jump of all.

It is only reasonable to assume that the higher circuits of the nervous system -- neurosomatic holistic awareness, neurogenetic evolutionary vision, metaprogramming flexibility -- are developing to allow us to cope with this deluge of higher information and potential higher coherence.

Toffler's Third Wave is only the sociological aspect of a mutation that is also biological and "spiritual."

We are going to live a lot longer than we have expected, and we are going to get a lot smarter.

A whole new reality will emerge from those mutations.

EXERCIZES

1. Make a list of ten areas in which your thinking-feeling is conservative. Guess how soon the world will change so totally that those ideas will seem not merely conservative but *irrelevant* (as the theological debates of 300 A.D. now seem irrelevant).

2. Make a list of ten areas in which your conceptualizing is radical. Guess how soon the world will change so totally that you will seem conservative in those areas.

3. Accept the longevity hypothesis. Imagine you are going to live at least 300 years. How much of that time do you want to spend loafing? How many different jobs would you like to work at? How many sports, arts or sciences you never had time for, would you then find the time to enjoy?

CHAPTER EIGHTEEN

THE NON-LOCAL QUANTUM CIRCUIT

The ways of the Creator are not our ways,
Mr. Deasy said. All history moves toward one
great goal, the manifestation of God.

James Joyce, Ulysses

A domesticated primate philosopher on an oxygen-supported carbon based planet circling a Type G star -- namely, the present author -- was once asked, "How do we think?"

"Well, we have a built-in bio-survival circuit which distinguishes nourishment-giving Things from predatory Things. . ."

"But can that circuit do *all* our thinking?"

"Well, no, but then there's an emotional-territorial circuit. . . "

"But, but, but -- "

"It's circuits-circuits-circuits all the way," I said.

What the Thinker thinks, the Prover proves.

We have made a beautiful (we hope beautiful) model of consciousness in terms of brain hardware and software. Now we need to remember again that, while the brain can be modeled by a computer, the model is never the whole system. The model-maker or metaprogrammer is bigger than the model or program.

In what are called "out of body experiences" (OOBEs) by parapsychologists, awareness *seems to* escape the confines of the nervous system entirely.

Such experiences are routinely triggered by advanced yoga practise, and they also occur spontaneously during what is called "near-death" or "clincal death" in which the patient appears to die, by all medical standards, but is revived by modern resuscitation techniques.

OOBEs also occur with heavy does of LSD and with ketamine, an anesthetic with strange psychedelic side-effects. They are also reported in shamanic traditions all over the world and by many "occultists" in our own society.

Example: One day in 1973, during a neuro-programming experiment, I "saw" something happening to my son at exactly that time in Arizona, over 500 miles away.

We can process this datum in various ways. We can say that my "astral body" actually traveled to Arizona; this is the occultist theory. We can more conservatively say that I developed extra-sensory-perception and "saw" Arizona without "going" there; there are many parapsychologists who prefer this third-circuit map of the 8th-Circuit experience. We can try to aver that I only "happened" to think of that scene while it was happening, by *synchronicity*; this is the Jungian approach. Or we can sweep it under the carpet by muttering "mere coincidence" or "sheer coincidence;" which is the traditional Rationalist approach.

We prefer to say, in accord with earlier writings of Timothy Leary

245

and the present author and the speculations of the Physics/Consciousness Research Group in San Francisco that such cases illustrate a special working of what is called in quantum mechanics Bell's Theorem.

Bell's Theorem is highly technical, but in ordinary language it amounts to something like this: There are no isolated systems; every particle in the universe is in "instantaneous" (faster-than-light) communication with every other particle. The Whole *System*, even the parts that are separated by cosmic distances, functions as a *Whole* System.

Now, such faster-than-light communication seems to be forbidden by Special Relativity, which makes a problem. Bell's Theorem, however, is inescapable: a theorem in physics is not a mere "theory"; it is a mathematical demonstration which *must be* true, if the mathematics contains no flaw, and if the experiments on which it is based are replicable. Bell's Theorem contains no mathematical flaw, and the experiments are replicable and have been replicated several times.

And yet we cannot dispense with Special Relativity either, because the mathematics there is equally iron and the experiments are legion that confirm it.

Two solutions have been proposed: and both assume that the "communication" involved in Bellian transmissions does not involve *energy,* since it is energy that cannot move faster than light. Dr. Edward Harris Walker suggests that what does move faster than light, and holds the Whole System together, is "consciousness." We may eventually be forced to accept this, in which case physics will have justified pantheism or at least panpsychism. The other alternative, proposed by Dr. Jack Sarfatti, is that the medium of Bellian transmissions is *information.*

Pure information, in the mathematical sense, does not require energy; it is that which orders energy. It is the negative of *entropy,* that which brings disorder to energy systems.

Dr. Sarfatti explains his theory as follows:

"Imagine that your brain is a computer, as modern neurology suggests. Now imagine that the whole universe is a big computer, *a mega-computer,* as John Lilly has proposed. Then imagine that the sub-quantum realm, the realm of what Dr. David Bohm calls 'hidden variables' is made up of *mini-mini-computers.* Now, the hardware of each 'computer' -- the universe, your brain, the sub-quantum mechanisms -- is localized. Each part of it is somewhere in spacetime, *here* not *there*, *now* not *then*. But the software -- the information -- is non-local. It is *here, there* and *everywhere; now, then* and *everywhen*.

The highest varieties of shamanic and yogic consciousness seem to begin from dilation beyond the immediate ("out-of-body-experience") and dilate, rapidly and dizzily, much further, to union with the smallest and the largest, the "Cosmic Mind" in short. This seems to be what would necessarily happen if the brain turned on to the non-local information system proposed by Sarfatti and implicit in Bell's Theorem.

The metaphysiological circuit, then, is this cosmic Information System. The synchronicities of circuits 5 to 7 are just the dawning notes of the symphony of all inter-related harmonies revealed to those who have experienced Circuit 8 in action. It is hard to avoid hyperbole when talking of such matters, but everything one can associate with the idea of Oneness With God is part of what is experienced in the vistas, beyond space-time, of this metaphysiological circuit.

Mystics stammer, gibber and rave incoherently in trying to discuss this. Beethoven says it for all of them, without words, in the fourth movement of the Ninth Symphony. The words of Schiller's "Ode to Joy," which Beethoven set to this virtually superhuman music, are a linear third circuit map conveying only a skeleton key to the multi-level meanings of the 8-circuit "language" of the melodic construction itself, which spans all consciousness from primitive bio-survival to metaphysiological cosmic fusion.

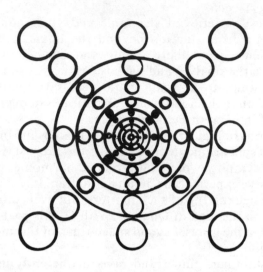

THE WHOLE SYSTEM IS A WHOLE SYSTEM

THE METAPHYSIOLOGICAL CIRCUIT

Wheels within wheels within wheels. . .
Dr. Sarfatti's computers within computers within computers. . .
Consciousness or information perceived as coherent intelligence expanding to infinity in all directions.

CHAPTER NINETEEN

PROMETHEUS
RISING

We are extending ourselves in Space and Time not *because* of capitalism or socialism but *in spite of* them. The Right/Left Capitalist/Socialist establishments are psychologically unprepared for our emerging situation in Time and Space.

F.M. Esfandiary, Upwingers

According to Patanjali, there are seven "limbs" to yoga, or as we would say seven steps or stages.

First is *asana*, which consists of holding a single posture (usually sitting) for prolonged periods of time. This is an attempt, in our terminology, to stabilize the bio-survival circuit by drowning it in monotony. You sit, and sit, and sit, and sit. Eventually, an "internal peace" is reached, which signifies the atrophying of all background levels of "unconscious" or unnoticed bio-survival anxiety.

In other schools, since *asana* is so monotonous and slow-working and because war (second-circuit mammalian struggles over territory) so common among domesticated primates, an alternative method of stabilizing the bio-survival circuit is used: martial arts. Akido, judo, karate etc. all emerged from yoga-like mystic schools, as bio-survival reprogrammers.

The second step in classical yoga, according to Patanjali, is *pranayama*. We have already commented on the efficiency of this breathing technique in quieting and mellowing-out second-circuit emotional programs.

(It will already be seen that yoga, like brainwashing, begins from the bottom up, working on the more primitive and older circuits first.)

The third step in yoga is *dharana* or *mantra. Dharana consists of concentrating on a single image, such as a vividly imagined red triangle, and ruthlessly pushing aside any other images, verbalizations or impressions that cross the mind's screen. In practise, this is beyond the powers of most students, so the majority of yoga teachers substitute mantra*, which is concentration (by repetition) on a single sentence, usually nonsensical, such as "Hare Krishna Hare Krishna Krishna Krishna Hare Hare" or "Aum Tat Sat Aum" or whatever.

Either practise, *dharana* or *mantra*, stops the third circuit "internal monologue," if persisted in for long enough periods each day.

The Western mystical equivalent is Cabala, the most complicated "Jewish joke" ever invented. Briefly, Cabala exhausts the third, semantic circuit by setting it to solve intractable numerological and verbal problems. The Far Eastern equivalent is the Zen *Koan*, which serves the same function in a less maniacally systematic way than Cabala, e.g. "What is the sound of one hand

251

clapping?" Zen koans are always combined with *zazen* (sitting Zen), which combines the first-circuit-clearing *asana* with second-circuit-mellowing breath-counting (a weaker *pranayama*).

When the student has acquired sufficient detachment from first-circuit anxieties, second-circuit emotions and third-circuit reality-maps, by way of *asana, pranayama* and *dharana* or *mantra*, Patanjali recommends the practise of *yama*. This includes, but is not limited to, celibacy. The ultimate of *yama* is to lose all interest in both the social and sexual aspects of the fourth circuit; to cease to care at all about family, tribal or societal matters. This is accomplished by self-denial, which is easier for those skilled in *asana, pranayama* and *dharana*, but still requires intense determination.

Some take a short-cut at this point, discovered after Patanjali or not known to him, by having themselves locked up in caves. Such isolation, as indicated eariler, helps vastly in bleaching out all four hominid circuits.

An alternative, for those not attracted to either celibacy or becoming hermits, is *Tantra,* invented in northern India around the time of Patanjali, This simply transmutes the fourth circuit by ceremonial, physiological and "magick" (self-hypnotic) explosion of the (prolonged) sexual act into fifth circuit neurosomatic rapture.

For those following the orthodox path of Patanjali, the fifth circuit is imprinted by *niyama*, which signifies "super-control" or "no-control," being the paradoxical state of *being spontaneous deliberately*. You cannot be taught *niyama*; you can only learn it by personal experience. We hypothesize that the bio-energies have to discharge somewhere, and then when one has driven them out of the first circuit by *asana*, out of the second circuit by *pranayama*, out of the third circuit by *dharana* or *mantra*, and out of the fourth circuit by *yama*, they are driven explosively upward into fifth circuit neurosomatic illumination.

The sixth step in yoga, according to Patanjali, is *dhyana*, which means "meditation" only in the roughest way. *Dhyana* means actually union with the object on the mind's screen, i.e. realization of the total meaning of the proposition that *mind and its contents are functionally identical*, i.e. opening the metaprogramming circuit. One can make *dhyana* on *anything*; yogis talk of making *dhyana* on a tree or a dog. just as Juan Matus, the Mexican shaman, talks of becoming one with a coyote or a star in the books of Castaneda.

The seventh step in yoga is *Samadhi*, from *sam*, (union; cognate of Greek *syn*) and *Adhis*, the Lord (cognate, Hebrew *Adonai* Greek *Adonis*). Here Patanjali and his successors are in violent dispute, some claiming there is only one *Samadhi*, others claiming two or three or many. Since this corresponds with the opening and imprinting of the neurogenetic circuit, we must opt for the opinion that there are many *Samadhi*, depending on which or how many of the Godly archetypes of the genetic archives are imprinted. Catholic mystics make *Samadhi* on the Virgin, Sufis on Allah, Aleister Crowley on Pan, etc; and, above all this, the eighth circuit cosmic information network can also be imprinted, making union not just with all sentient beings and some emblematic archetype of the DNA master program, but with the inorganic universe as well. It was from this second order or metaphysiological Samadhi that Gandhi said, "God is in the rock, too -- *in the rock!*" and pantheists of all sorts, in all traditions, emphatically agree with Candadian psychiatrist, R.M. Bucke who said after his own 8th Circuit Samadhi that the universe "is not a dead machine but a living presence."

This planet is, to put the matter baldly, populated and largely controlled by domesticated primates who are not in all respects reasonable men and women. Voltaire may have been exaggerating when he said that to understand the mathematical meaning of infinity, consider the extent of human stupidity; but the situation is almost that bad. Millions have been murdered by stupid leaders or stupid mobs, for stupid reasons, in every century; and the bizarre (accidentally imprinted) reality-tunnels which make this possible continue to rule us and robotize us.

Nor is stupidity the exclusive possession of one group or another; you do not need a "vocation" for it as you do for the priesthood. It seems to be a contagious socio-semantic disturbance which afflicts all of us at one time or another. Notorious examples can be found in the lives of the great. As we have already mentioned an exact measurement of the extent of stupidity among the learned is provided by the fact that every scientific revolution takes one generation. Elderly scientists hardly ever accept a new theory, however good it is, and the revolution is only completed when a second generation, free of the old imprints, with vulnerable neurons, imprints the new reality-map.

But if science, the paradigm of rationality, is infested with enough stupidity to cause this general one-generation time-lag, what can we say of politics, economics and religion? Time-lags of thousands of years seem to be "normal" in these areas. Indeed, it was through contemplation of religious history that Voltaire was led to his conclusion that human stupidity approximates to the infinite. The study of politics is hardly more inspiring. Let us just summarize the matter by saying that stupidity has murdered and imprisoned more geniuses (and more ordinary people), burned more books, slaughtered more populations, and blocked progess more effectively than any other force in history.

It may be no exaggeration to say that stupidity has killed more people than all the diseases known to medicine and psychiatry.

Intelligence is the capacity to receive, decode and transmit information efficiently. Stupidity is blockage of this process at any point. Bigotry, ideologies etc. block the ability to receive; robotic reality-tunnels block the ability to decode or integrate new signals; censorship blocks transmission.

If intelligence could be increased, obviously solutions could be found more quickly to the various Doomsday scenarios threatening us.

If each scientist working on the energy-resources problem could double or triple his or her intelligence, work that would require 20 years might be done in six.

If human stupidity in general decreased, there would be less opposition to original thinking and new approaches to our old problems, less censorship and less bigotry.

If stupidity decreased, less money would be wasted on vast organized imbecilities such as the Arms Race, and more would be available for life enhancing projects.

There is nothing rationally desirable that cannot be achieved sooner if rationality itself increases. This is virtually a tautology, but we must consider the corollary:

Work to achieve Intelligence Intensification is work to achieve all our other sane and worthwhile goals.

Maurice Nicholl, physician, psychiatrist, student of Jung, Gurdjieff and Esoteric Christianity, wrote that "the only purpose in work on consciousness is to decrease the amount of violence in the world." This is Public Health Problem Number One in the nuclear age, the age of overkill.

We are not talking about mere increase in linear I.Q. -- third circuit semantic cleverness. We are talking of also the kinds of right-brain intelligence that Nicoll aquired from Jungian neurogenetic research and Gurdjieff's metaprogramming techniques. We are talking of, say, Beethoven's intelligence, which so disturbed Lenin, who could not bear to listen to the *Appassionata* (Sonata 23) because it made him want to weep "and pat people on the head, and we mustn't pat them on the head, we must hit them on the head, hit them hard, and make them obey." More of Beethoven's intelligence is needed, desperately, to create a signal that the current Lenins cannot ignore, that will make them weep, and stop hitting heads.

We need more mentations, less munitions. The second-circuit mammalian political games are a million years obsolete.

Dr. Nathan Kline has predicted that, within 21 years, we will have drugs to improve memory, drugs to erase unpleasant memories, drugs to increase or decrease any emotion, drugs to prolong or shorten childhood, etc. It takes no great imagination to foresee that such chemicals will allow us greater control over our neural tunnel-realities than ever before. Obviously. people will *use and abuse* these potions in many ways, but the most intelligent will use them in *the most intelligent way*, namely to increase and intensify their intelligence in every direction possible on our spectrum of 8 circuits. Chiefly, they will use them to increase neurological freedom, to debug and reprogram obsolete reality-maps, to generally expand consciousness and sensitivity to signals and information.

The potential for a neurological revolution -- planetary Intelligence Intensification -- should be quite clear to anyone who has even a slight knowledge of so primitive a psychedelic as LSD. One of the least known facts about the LSD research in the 1960s was that the longest single research project with LSD, at Spring Grove Hospital, Maryland, showed an average 10% increase in linear IQ alone as well as the metaprogramming vistas and neurogenetic awakenings popularized by the outlaw LSD culture and its gurus.

And there is a direct feedback loop between neuropharmacology and other brain sciences. As William Burroughs says, "Anything that can be done chemically can be done by other means. " Yoga plus bio-feedback produces detachment from old imprints quicker than yoga alone; hypnotism and mind-drugs produce synergetically more than either produces without the other; John Lilly has duplicated LSD effects in his isolation tanks; etc.

It is commonplace for alarmists to warn us that the full armory of synergetically interacting neurosciences now evolving will allow unscrupulous tyrants to brainwash us more totally than ever before.

We need to realize that the same technology, wisely used by intelligent men and women, can free us from every form of neurotic and irrational rigidity, to dial and focus our nervous systems as easily as we dial or focus our TV, turning any channel or circuit off and on as we choose. This is what metaprogramming (cybernetic) consciousness means.

Why be depressed when you can be happy, dumb when you can be smart, agitated when you can be tranquil? Obviously, most people are depressed, dumb and agitated most of the time because they *lack the tools* to repair and correct damaged, defective circuits in their nervous system. We are acquiring the tools, and this Intelligence Intensification has the Pleasure Principle to fuel it. That is, the more internal freedom you achieve, the more you want. It is more fun to be happy than sad, more enjoyable to choose your emotions than to have them inflicted upon you by mechanical glandular processes, more pleasurable to solve your problems than to be stuck with them forever.

In brief, Intelligence Intensification means intelligence-studying-intelligence (I^2), and the first thing discovered by intelligence-studying-intelligence (the brain studying the brain: metaprogramming) is that the more types of intelligence you have, the more fun it is to try to develop even more subtle, sensitive, futique levels of awareness; higher intelligence still.

In summary, Intelligence Intensification is desirable, because there is not a single problem confronting humanity that is not either caused or considerably worsened by the prevailing stupidity (insensitivity) of the species: badly wired robots bumping into and maiming and killing each other.

Intelligence Intensification is attainable, because modern advances in neuroscience are showing us how to alter any imprinted, conditioned or learned reflex, that previously restricted us.

Intelligence Intensification is hedonic, because the more free-dom and consciousness you achieve, the more you want; the less willing you are to slip back to dumb, blind, mechanistic circuits.

Intelligence Intensification can accelerate our progress toward abolition of war and poverty; find cures for cancer and schizoph-renia; achieve space migration and life extension (giving us space enough and time enough to achieve even more cosmic levels of awareness); or accomplish any other worthwhile goals.

Like death and poverty, stupidity has been around so long that people cannot imagine human life without it, but it is rapidly becoming obsolete. However many special interest groups (intel-ligence agencies so-called, advertisers, tyrants, clergy, etc.) may profit from stupidity, humanity as a whole will profit more for its abolition.

Approximately 50% of the human race has not evolved fully into the third circuit yet. That is, although they can exchange primitive signals and handle primitive artifacts, they are still mostly operating on the mammalian emotional circuit and the pre-mammalian bio-survival circuit.

Ronald Reagan is their current leader in the U.S. Third circuit types cannot understand this and regard it as sinister, but it is simple mammalian herd-behavior. Reagan is the typical primate leader; the noises he makes, which appear meaningless to the third circuit Rationalist, are urgently meaningful to the territiorial-emotional-patriotic minds of the majority of primates.

Another 20% are "responsible, intelligent adults" with fully developed third and fourth circuits. They spend most of their time *worrying*, because the predominantly primate parameters of human society seem absurd, immoral and increasingly dangerous to them.

Another 20% are neurosomatic adepts. Fourth-circuit Moral-ists denounce them as "mystics," "space cases," "nuts," "the Me generation," "irresponsible hedonists," etc.

Most of the fifth circuit adepts (aquarian conspirators) have learned Joyce's arts of "silence, exile, cunning": they are invisible. Others have turned their talents to "faith-healing" or various occult gimmicks of that sort, and very carefully do not tell their clients that the local ideology, morality and reality-tunnel is what made them ill in the first place. They give "good energy" and sensibly avoid conflict with the moral ideological "authorities."

Another 5% have neurogenetic consciousness, and function as Evolutionary Agents -- servants of the Life Force, in Shaw's terminology. Their "God" is Pan (life), and their goal is immortality.

Another 3% have mastered the metaprogramming circuit and make up what Gurdjieff called "the Conscious Circle of humanity." They are *Free Masons*, in the original meaning of that debased term: co-creators of future realities.

Only 2% are neuro-quantum adepts and beyond space-time categories entirely.

All these estimates are approximations.

The newer circuits (neurosomatic bliss, neurogenetic "Atman" consciousness, metaprogramming reality-games, non-local "cosmic" awareness) must have *some* function.

We can only assume they are preparing us for our new situation in space-time, after Space colonization, after longevity and immortality, after the Acceleration Factor accelerates even faster.

Engineers rate an engine in revolutions-per-second. Looking at human history in terms of this metaphor we clearly see that:

In the Old Stone Age, the acceleration factor was just slowly beginning to operate. We could estimate change then in, perhaps, revolutions per 10,000 years.

With the neolithic revolution and urbanization soon after, the pace began to pick up. We can speak from that point on in terms of revolutions-per-millennium.

After Galileo, revolutions-per-century became the normal rate of change.

In this century we have moved into revolutions-per-generation.

We are now obviously moving into an acceleration of revolutions-per-decade.

By the time the Consciousness Revolution peaks, the Longevity Pill is widely available, cloning is normal and all the ideas in the book, including the most wild and radical ones, seem quaint and old-fashioned -- i.e. about 1995 -- we will probably be growing accustomed to thinking in terms of revolutions-per-year.

There is no reason to accept the tunnel-reality of this book as final. If you really understand the message, you will invent a bigger and better Future than I have suggested. As Barbara Marx Hubbard says:

THE FUTURE EXISTS FIRST IN IMAGINATION, THEN IN WILL, THEN IN REALITY.

APPENDIX

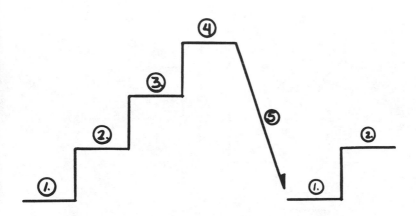

The neurogenetic script, cyclical aspect:

1. The helpless infant (Circuit I).
2. The walking-struggling-competing child (Circuit II).
3. The word-and-tool-using older child (Circuit III).
4. Imprinting-conditioning the sexual circuit (IV) into domesticated parenthood.
5. Reproduction and. . . the cycle continues. . .

". . . their weatherings and their marryings and their buryings and their natural selections. ."
                                                    Joyce, Finnegans Wake

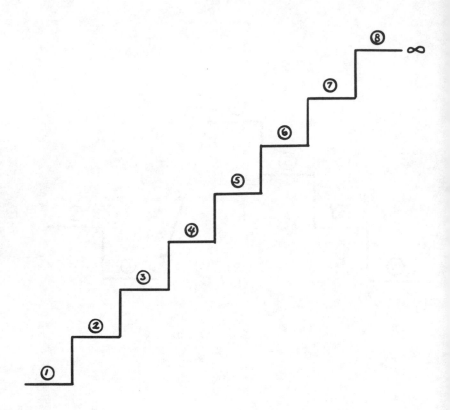

The neurogenetic script, upward-spiraling aspect:

1. Primitive organisms; recapitulated in infancy.
2. Vertebrate struggle, recapitulated in childhood.
3. Semantic-technological learning, recapitulated in school.
4. Socio-sexual domesticity.
5. Neurosomatic rapture, pre-capitulating zero-gravity and Space Migration.
6. Neurogenetic vision, pre-capitulating Longevity-Immortality.
7. Metaprogramming skill, pre-capitulating Intelligence Intensification.
8. Metaphysiological cosmic vision, pre-capitulating. . . WHAT?